'If you ... about the
survival ... spirit, and good lives being forged
from the most unfortunate origins, then *But We All Shine On* is

— John Niven, author of *Kill Your Friends*

'It could be said that family is a collection of disputed memories between one group of people over a lifetime. But for the child in care this "one group" of people is continually dispersed to the point of being impossible to recognise themselves. A non-family of shadows. With his pen Paolo projects light on the darkest path as he seeks the family that never was and unravels a tragic, comical, magical and moving story. All we are is our story. Without it we are pages of spurious ellipses. We need Paolo Hewitt with his torch. Shine on, Paolo Hewitt. Shine on.'

– Lemn Sissay MBE, writer

'Reading these remarkably personal and inspirational self-discovery journeys bought a mixture of emotions that were both a joy and painful to feel. It never ceases to amaze me, the strength and humanity which stays secure within hurt children and lives with them forever. A beautifully written memoir which has to be read and recognised for the achievement it is and the dignity it deserves.'

– Hope Daniels, care leaver and author of *Hackney Child*

'This book will put tears in your eyes and leave you with a smile on your face. It is a testament to the spirit of five boys who are forced to confront fear, loneliness and varying degrees of mental and physical cruelty, yet emerge as strong, decent men. Paolo Hewitt draws the stories of his four orphanage friends together with great integrity, splashing poetry and light over their shared trauma. Reading *But We All Shine On* is a humbling, uplifting experience. It is a worthy companion to the author's brilliant memoir *The Looked After Kid*.'

– John King, author of *The Football Factory* and *Human Punk*

'Paolo writes with such deftness of touch and fondness for the real-life characters that populate this engaging memoir that the reader is taken into their lives and hearts; he opens a door and invites us into the world of the "care" system in the 1970s. Rightly, he makes us feel sad for the many, many children who suffered cruelty or indifference at the hands of people who were meant to care for them, but this is no misery memoir. Paolo doesn't dwell in the darkness or want us to – he shows us how so often the human spirit survives and triumphs over ill-treatment, rejection and abandonment, against all odds. He has no interest in pandering to the voyeuristic schadenfreude of readers who hungrily devour graphic accounts of child abuse; instead, he gives us hope, humour and warmth. Traumatic and poignant events are recounted factually and simply without the trappings of melodrama, but are all the more affecting for that. His tone is honest and humane; he seeks to understand and forgive the wrongs done to him and others and tries to avoid judgement. In passing, he contrasts the experience of young people in care then and now, and even for those of us who know only too well that the system is still deeply flawed, the book serves as a reminder of how far we have come as a society in terms of how we treat our most vulnerable children.'

– Natasha Finlayson, Chief Executive,
The Who Cares? Trust

'Reflecting on care in the not-too-distant past through the eyes of children, *But We All Shine On* gives insight into where we've come from, and challenges where we are and where we still need to go. It can help get us to the better future we all desire for children in care. In the created family of the children's home, relationships matter – they can change and sustain a person for a lifetime, and bring the opportunities of life to be lived.'

– Jonathan Stanley, National Centre for
Excellence in Residential Child Care

'Hewitt has shed a light on the murky world of late '60s and early '70s children's homes. An empathetic listener and master story teller his is the authentic voice…from the inside…first hand. The characters are his friends. They trust him. The stories herein are touching, funny and most of all redemptive. It's quite possibly his masterpiece.'

– Dr. Robert, The Blow Monkeys

But We All Shine On

by the same author

The Looked After Kid
My Life in a Children's Home
Paolo Hewitt
ISBN 978 1 84905 588 8
eISBN 978 1 78450 042 9

of related interest

No Matter What
An Adoptive Family's Story of Hope, Love and Healing
Sally Donovan
ISBN 978 1 84905 431 7
eISBN 978 0 85700 781 0

Shattered Lives
Children Who Live with Courage and Dignity
Camila Batmanghelidjh
ISBN 978 1 84310 603 6
eISBN 978 1 84642 254 6

But We All Shine On

The Remarkable Orphans of Burbank Children's Home

Paolo Hewitt

Jessica Kingsley *Publishers*
London and Philadelphia

First published in 2015
by Jessica Kingsley Publishers
73 Collier Street
London N1 9BE, UK
and
400 Market Street, Suite 400
Philadelphia, PA 19106, USA

www.jkp.com

Library of Congress Cataloging in Publication Data
Hewitt, Paolo, 1958-
But we all shine on : the remarkable orphans of
Burbank Children's Home / Paolo Hewitt.
pages cm
ISBN 978-1-84905-583-3 (alk. paper)
1. Foster children--United States--Biography. 2. Orphanages--United States. I. Title.
HV881.H49 2015
362.73092'279493--dc23
2014014550

British Library Cataloguing in Publication Data
A CIP catalogue record for this book is available from the British Library

ISBN 978 1 84905 583 3
eISBN 978 1 78450 033 7

Printed and bound in Great Britain

I dedicate this book to Des, Norman, David and Terry and to all the children who lived at Burbank Children's Home. I hope you all find the light I did, given to me by Dio and shaped by Sahika.

Contents

Acknowledgements

Thank you to Iain Munn who first took on this work and then graciously passed it onto Stephen Jones and the fine people at Jessica Kingsley Publishers, without a fuss. Here's to Dundee F.C.

Thank you George Georgiou for being such a great Academy graduate and for your help in designing the cover. Here's to your wife Jenny as well. Thank you Simon Wells, thank you Kathy and Tim Pring, thank you Johnny, Inki, Stirling and Asa Chandler, thank you Peter, Kin Lin and Talia, thank you Dennis Dervish, and all those I meet under the Tree of Spurs, thank you to all the Park Lane End boys and girls, thank you Il Nipperoni, thank you Katherine and Keith, thank you Guy, thank you Eugene and Nicky, thank you Dylan, Gareth and Penny, thank you David Luxton and Rebecca Winfield, thank you Gavin Martin, thank you Imran, Arfan, Munnie, Sweetie, Reshi, Wayde, Anaia, Kaizen and Jaienna, thank you Irvine and Elizabeth, thank you Father Sean Carroll, thank you Sister Patricia, thank you all at St Peter-in-Chains Church, thank you Sheas, Jonesy and the Stone Foundation boys, thank you Rob, Michelle, Joe and Cleo, thank you Mark Powell, thank you John King, thank you Pete G and all the Woking boys and girls, thank you Mark and Anita, thank you Ant, Anna and Lucky, thank you

Paisan Kevin, thank you George Russo, thank you deeply, Nina and Francesca, plus all the Yeovil contingent, especially the four angels, Izzy, Millie, Evie and Abi, thank you so much Stephen Jones and all at Jessica Kingsley Publishers, thank you Tony Marchant, thank you Johnny Harris, thank you Russell and Joanne, thank you Christopher Makris, and thank you Phil and Richard for the state we are in.

Prologue

I climbed aboard the silver bird to India and awoke on a beach in Goa. Before me, the sea glimmered in seven different shades of blue. Sunlight created row upon row of small, sparkling jewels which then danced upon the sea's white flecked tiny waves.

I ran and immersed myself in this gift from above.

I was exhausted. I had spent the last year writing a book called *The Looked After Kid*, a memoir about my unhappy childhood and subsequent teenage life spent in a children's home called Burbank, and writing that book had taken everything out of me.

Moreover, it was a book I had waited to write. The idea of writing the book had occurred to me whilst I was in my twenties. The excitement that thought first engendered was quickly tempered by another voice, a more insistent voice, which insisted that I put the book on hold until I was mature enough to write it.

That voice was correct. Although there was a part of me that wanted to rush in print, it was incumbent upon me to wait until the deep smoke of confusion had cleared from my soul. Then, only then, could I write with a deeper and better perspective.

It was too simple for me to show you how my foster mother had pushed me into a cupboard and locked the door. I needed to show you *why* she did that.

To do so I would have to grow as a person and at the same time immerse myself in my craft. I downed tools and waited.

When I did come to write *The Looked After Kid*, it happened naturally. I had finished my two biographies of the band Oasis and wanted to get away from the music world.

I got up one morning, followed my regular routine and, suddenly, I was writing about my past. Moreover, I was doing so with true freedom, with no fear or compunction about what I was doing or where the book was heading. Those two elements sustained me throughout the whole work.

The story began with my birth and removal from my mother's arms after just two days on this earth. My mother had lived in England for eleven years and for many years I wondered why my mother would leave Sorrento, a town filled with brilliant colour, and unusual warmth and smiles, for the grey of England.

Then I read Norman Lewis's wonderful book, *Naples 44*, read of the diseases and the famine and the vice that the war had created, and knew then why my mother had fled.

My mother arrived in this country in 1947. Soon, she was living through one of the coldest winters of the century. Furthermore, the British still despised the Italians for their part in the Second World War and so extended no friendship towards her. She was isolated.

My mother had two children, Nina and Francesca, and then, in 1952, suffered a major breakdown. Despite his efforts, Mr Hewitt, their father, could not save her and she was admitted to a hospital in Couldson Surrey. Sometime in 1957 she lay with someone and that someone was my father. To this day I have not met him. I do not know his name or his nationality. For I had been born in a thunderstorm and knew not the source of my lightning.

The hospital covered up the incident and my mother could not help.

Her memory by now had been obliterated by drugs and what was left of it she did not want to waste on unhappy dreams. So she pulled on her ever present cigarettes, the only moments of pleasure in her wasted days and dressed in a pink cardigan with a blur striped t-shirt and light blue skirt, and she looked at me and said of my father, 'His name was Mr Cruise. I can't tell you any more. Sorry, Paolo, sorry,' and those words broke my heart.

One day, a woman came and took me away from the nursery. Her name was Mrs K. Mrs K. was a vindictive, unhappy woman who broke my childhood in a million different ways. And then broke it some more. She beat me so deeply, both emotionally and physically, that it would take me at least twenty years to recover from the relentless assault she made upon my character, my soul.

Her cruelty, her anger, her indifference, her lack of any love or compassion towards me or the world, disabled me emotionally. I became extremely fearful and deeply scared of the world. I became shy, a compulsive worrier, a boy with no address, no identity.

When I was ten Mrs K. decided that she had had enough of me. She put me back into care.

My first children's home was called Woodrough, situated in Bramley near Guildford. I got there in April of 1968 and within a month, I knew happiness for the very first time. Woodrough was run by a couple, John and Molly Brown, and they created a home which should be the model for all children's homes. Of the many things they did for me (and so many others), they made me feel special, made me feel wanted, made me feel that I had importance.

Of course, happiness was not to be, so in August of that same year I was transferred to Burbank Children's Home in Woking, Surrey. Although in later life I spent many years running from Burbank, I now began to see the positive effect it had had on me.

As I delved deep into my mind, for the first time, I saw, I *felt*, the strength us kids drew from each other in those days of ours, as we navigated our way through life as orphans, trying so very hard to understand the rich but perplexing strangeness of our lives.

I looked back and where once I saw darkness, now I saw light and hope and strength, and it was that which I tried to convey to the reader, that the Children's Home, *my* children's home, was tinged with blackness but it also had light, colour, and adventure.

I finished the book on a positive note. The day after I awoke and knew I needed rest, I needed healing.

Hence, my arrival in Goa.

By the time I had settled in that wonderful part of the world, I had come to a major decision. I had decided that the book I had just written would never see the light of day. I would not allow it to be published. Of that I became certain.

The work was too raw, too open. People would not understand it. For years, I had kept my past a closely guarded secret and I was not yet ready to blow my cover.

With that decided, I settled into Goa. I rose early with the sun, went swimming with the jewels. I sat in a hammock and read about Tolstoy. At night, I ate well, made friends, watched football, slept beautifully.

Within two weeks, I had recovered from my labours.

So had my mind.

Five months later, *The Looked After Kid* was published to great acclaim. The reviews were uniformly positive; people seemed genuinely moved by what I had written. E-mails started coming in extolling the book's virtues.

One arrived from a girl in Liverpool. It read, 'I hate you. It is four in the morning and I have to go to work at seven but I can't put your bloody book down.'

I was thrilled by the response. It felt like I had entered a new era as a new person. People who once harboured serious reservations about me, now extended the hand of friendship.

I took it gladly.

Others said to me, 'It must have been so cathartic, writing that book,' and I smiled and I said yes, it was. But I was lying. It was the act of *publishing* the book that liberated me, not the writing of it.

The day that book came into being I told the whole world something I had found impossible to do previously – that I was an orphan.

In *The Looked After Kid*, I revealed everything I had kept hidden all those years. I had only told a handful of people – if that – about my past. I feared sympathy. I suspected I had a touch of talent for writing and I did not want to be judged through the prism of compassion.

The book then was my way of coming out – and the relief was tremendous. No more hiding my past from others, no more deception, no more changing the conversations at friends' when the subject of parents or childhood came up.

Instead, freedom, the freedom of definition, a move towards a real identity, one which had strength and endurance, one which gave me roots. This was my past, and this is who I am because of it.

Then, excitement. The BBC wanted to create a series about care that would go right across their network. There would be films, documentaries, radio shows on the subject.

I travelled in for a meeting. I met high-powered executives. A documentary about life after care with myself and others was put into motion.

Many good things happened around this documentary but perhaps the best thing of all was that they tracked down the phone numbers of many of the people I once shared Burbank Children's Home with.

Top of the list was the number for Des Hurrion. I was thrilled to be given his information.

Des was my closest friend at the Home. For much of our time at Burbank, we were inseparable, two boys drawn together by humour and music and football and a shared attitude towards life.

I called Des. He came on the line and we spoke as if no time had passed between us. A week later, I met him at a pub in Hammersmith.

Alcohol was consumed, a great friendship renewed. At eleven that night we parted, both of us swaying dangerously into the night.

I realised on the way home that half of my high came just from being re-united with this man.

The next day I awoke with a smile – and a hangover. I turned on the computer.

More e-mails about *The Looked After Kid* had arrived.

One guy had written to inform me that he had sent my book to a friend of his who, like me, had grown up in a children's home.

He wrote, 'I sent him your book four days ago. He has just called to say, "This book is me, this book is me!" You should be proud of yourself.'

Then another e-mail arrived and it was from a Norman Bass. I opened this with great interest.

I had spent many years with Norman at Burbank. Although we had not been close, he had been a permanent fixture in my life at an important time. Now, after a million years, he was back in touch.

This always happened around the writing or publication of a book: people you needed to see suddenly appeared as if summoned by mysterious forces. First Des, now Norman. The process never failed and I never questioned it.

Norman wrote that he had thoroughly enjoyed my book. He added that he would be in London soon and did I want to meet up?

Of course, I did. Of course.

On the morning of our appointment, as I sat on the train, I tried to recall Norman's face. It was a fruitless task. His features somehow eluded me. When I met him later that day, I found out why.

Even though he had been at Burbank for five years, Norman had spent most of his time running away. That is why I could not remember his features. He was always on the run.

As he greeted me with a warm handshake, I noted that he was tall, suited, wore glasses, had receding hair, was well built, authoritative in nature, and quite controlled. Not what I had expected at all. Which begged the question – what had I expected?

And I could not answer that question either.

'Come on,' said Norman, 'I know a place we can eat.'

He had chosen a pub for lunch, a place where suited men and women from nearby offices took their lunch break and talked earnestly to each other over beer and steak pies.

Norman, with his suit and tie and briefcase, blended right in. I, with my bright Gabicci top and white Levi jeans, did not.

We settled in our chairs, began talking. Chit chat at first, pleasantries. And then a rush of words, the pouring out and sharing of memories, a recall of our time at Burbank, the kids, the staff members, the characters around Woking town.

The conversation was seamless. Two hours seemed to pass in an hour.

Reluctantly, Norman looked at his watch. 'Got a train to catch,' he said, apologetically.

'That's a shame,' I said in earnest. We left the pub and headed back to London Bridge station.

At the bottom of the escalators I shook hands with Norman.

'I'll be in touch,' I said and I meant it.

After he had gone, I jumped a train. As I rattled and rolled through the underground, dark foreboding walls either side of me, one question kept presenting itself to me. Why had it been so easy between us? Why had there been no awkward moments as I had expected?

After all, the odds had been seriously against us getting on.

Norman and I had not been close during our days at Burbank. He was younger than me and, at that time, all I was interested in were the big boys of the Home, the ones who carried themselves confidently, smoked ciggies, kissed girls, played football.

Moreover, Norman did not share my passion for books, music and football. We were miles apart.

Yet none of that mattered today. Why?

The Children's Home is why.

Burbank had twinned us for life. Norman and I had survived care. We had crossed the same stormy sea and finished intact on the other side.

That feat alone had bound us together and, yes, bound us like brothers.

The writer Arthur Miller once wrote of his wife, Marilyn Monroe, an alumna of care, that she could walk into a room and spot a fellow orphan straight away.

It was the longing in their eyes that she instinctively recognised.

I did not have that power but what Miller said of Monroe resonated with me.

There is a level of strong, psychic understanding between all care kids – and that is what I had felt with Norman that day. Both of us had spotted the longing in each other's eyes.

When I got home and settled, I took the thought further. If Norman and I were brothers of a kind, then it stood to reason that I had an entire other family. They were not blood related; they were not close to me. Instead, they were the children of Burbank, the children I grew up with during the most crucial period in my life.

Their names and faces now appeared before me.

Jimmy B. for example. When I first arrived at the Home, he protected me. He saw I was confused, a frightened boy. He understood I needed to be toughened up.

Jimmy taught me to fight. He made me punch walls so that my knuckles would harden. Because of Jimmy, I defended myself well against those who sought to physically harm me.

This was good.

He also nicknamed me Bert (after my middle name Alberto) because he couldn't pronounce Paolo properly.

This was bad. Especially when it came to girls.

'What's your name?'

'Paolo.'

A little shiver.

'Ooh, that's a nice name. Is it…'

'Oi Bert, you coming or what?'

End of romance.

Colin N. introduced me to the music of Jimi Hendrix and taught me how to laugh at authority instead of shaking all over every time I encountered it.

Grahame B. first instilled in me the value of dressing well, of looking good despite a life you lived to the contrary.

Frank and Jimmy welcomed me into their gang, made me feel wanted, something the adult world had conspicuously failed to do up until that point in my life.

As their faces appeared before me, I began wondering about their lives. What had happened to them? Did they make it through the hoop okay? Had the Gods smiled upon them or banished them to the gutter?

My first thought was to fear for them. After care, many children snapped in two. It is said that every year, forty per cent of care kids go through prison; sixty per cent end up homeless. Just thirteen per cent a year pass GSCE exams.

A tiny percentage have become rich or famous – the actress Marilyn Monroe, the designer Bruce Oldfield, the footballer John Fashnau, the actress Samantha Morton, and the prophet Muhammad sprang to mind – but many fell by the wayside.

Certainly, my generation had huge mountains placed in front of them.

At that time kids as young as sixteen, were thrown into the wider world without any support of any kind. They had not been programmed to navigate the difficult road ahead. No one had taught them the basics of living. No one saw to it that they found accommodation or work. No one thought of their emotional well-being.

They had been sent out to face the lions alone, without any protection whatsoever.

Scandalous.

How then had the kids from my Home fared?

The only way to answer that question was to track my people down. But how? The answer came instinctively. Trust the process. Start the book and they will come to you. Des and Norman already had.

Within a month of Norman e-mailing me, two men, who I had grown up with at Burbank, had been in touch.

Their names were Terry Hodgson and David Westbrook.

Terry I had known for about a year at Burbank. He frightened the life out of me with his size and latent aggression.

David was a cheeky little kid who was much younger than me but who, never the less, I befriended towards the end of my stay.

So I made arrangements to see all of them. I would now go on a journey to see where life had taken my brothers. Who would I first approach?

Easy.

Des Hurrion, of course, once my bestest friend in the whole wide world.

One

Author in Search of a Character

The Story of Des Hurrion

On the silver snake to meet Des, I thought about how children in care rarely talked to each other about their fractured past, their torn up history.

Certainly that was the case at Burbank.

I knew Des Hurrion closely for five years and I never knew why I shared a home with him. He never told me his circumstances. I never told him mine.

Perhaps, we were not emotionally mature enough to do so. Or – and this I think is closer to the mark – we just accepted that life had badly twisted our fortunes, and that words were not necessary. We were in Burbank, we were in care, we had been floored.

What else could we do but try to get up?

Now, thirty years later, I was about to find out why Des lived with me at Burbank.

Des met me off the train. He wore a black coat, black trousers and shoes. His colours in no way mitigated the excitement that was palpable between us.

We now knew that come what may, we would be in each other's lives until forever.

It was a good feeling.

Still, I was slightly uneasy. I wanted to ask Des a question, a question I could not ask him when we had first met in Hammersmith. That night, it would not have been appropriate, it would have been out of context.

Now, I wanted to see if Des could deliver the answer I sought.

I needed to ask Des about his affair with Julie, the married woman who ran our Home. Julie had taken Des away from me. He had been mine and then he became hers. I needed to know why and how that had happened.

Des and I walked to the nearby Chinese restaurant. When we entered, it was a quarter full, perfect for my needs.

Not too far away from where we sat was Des's rented house where he spent his time writing sitcom scripts.

This had been his work for years but soon it would stop. His production company had just dropped him. None of his projects had got off the ground and the money he had been using to fund his writing was now dwindling.

'I'll finish the script I am working on at the moment,' he said nonchalantly, 'and then I will find another job. Probably get a quiet office job and do writing in my spare time.'

Des betrayed no bitterness at having to give up this work. Since leaving Burbank, he had lived in many places, worked at many jobs. These included barman, postman and IT manager.

In that sense, he had been much braver than me.

I've always been filled with an ambition directed towards a writing life. To be employed as anything else would, in my eyes, mark me as a burning failure.

Des was different. He marched to his own drum beat, cared not for the gossip of others. He would work as anything – and he did.

I told him that script-writing was the job I thought him perfect for.

He smiled, a little embarrassed. But it was true.

Des was not only the funniest boy at Burbank during my time there but he was easily the brightest, the most imaginative.

If you would have put money on anyone from the Burbank class of 1970 succeeding in life, Des Hurrion was the one you would have bet on.

He had an enviable intelligence. He once told me that at the age of ten he decided to teach himself French and Latin, which he duly did.

I wasn't surprised at this achievement. Nothing seemed beyond his ken.

During the first three years of his stay at Burbank, Des attended a private school in Nottingham.

I have met and worked with many privately educated men but Des was not like any of them; he never used his intelligence as a sword, to wound or cut down others. He was not vindictive.

His was a graceful, generous intelligence, shot through with a warm wit that appealed to everyone in the Home, and I mean everyone.

From staff member to the youngest child, no one was exempted from Des Hurrion's many charms.

Des contained a self-assurance that for a shy fearful boy like me was thoroughly addictive. It still is. I have always envied people who appeared self-possessed, confident, looked like they knew exactly what they were doing in life, their faces seemingly untroubled by the world.

I keenly noted them on London tubes and buses, on the street, in work places, in shops, in clubs, in cafés and restaurants, and I yearned for just a smidgen of their self-possession. I thought, if I could just have a little of their magic and then my world will be a beautiful place to live in. And on such notions do fools build their castles.

At Burbank, Des made me feel that anything was possible, that despite living in care, the future was mine to mould into whatever shape I so desired. He shrugged off limitations. He did not even acknowledge them.

How I loved him for that. How I envied him for that.

Then Julie seduced him and he was no longer mine. Once I had a hundred per cent of Des. Now, I only had fifty.

I have handled many difficult things in life but rejection burns me like nothing else.

Yet, I couldn't blame Des.

That song Bobby Goldsborough used to sing on the radio to Des and me about loving an older woman in summer, said it all. He was seventeen and she was thirty-five. Who could resist? I would have done exactly the same.

The affair lasted months and only I knew about it.

Certainly, Barry, Julie's husband didn't, or he would have torn the Home down, brick by brick.

Des even shacked up with Julie for a while. This was after she and Barry had split up for good and he had moved far away. But it didn't last. How could it? The thrill had gone.

Suddenly, they no longer worried about being caught in compromising positions. Now they worried about mortgages and jobs, the nine to five life.

Des was never cut out for that existence. He still isn't.

Thinking about this now, perhaps there was another reason for hunting Des down, a selfish reason. Perhaps by simply being with him I thought I would once again feel my future turning gold, see the world opening up in front of my eyes, just as it did back in my youth when Des and I sat together in the sitting room and played records, or talked in the garden, sitting there with a ball at our feet, the sun placed high above us in a careless blue sky.

'I'm still not sure,' he said carefully, 'if I should tell you everything about my life and what happened, but because it is you,' he ruefully smiled, 'I probably will.'

Forty-nine years old now, Des retained a face that time had rendered quite keen. His dark hair was pushing back a bit but that just served to emphasise his large brown eyes. The skin around those eyes remained relatively unwrinkled and his constant expression was one of being slightly amazed by what was going on around him. When you discovered what he had been through as child and man, that was no big surprise.

I pushed the tape recorder across towards him.

'What better time than now to start the talk?' I said.

'What better time indeed?' he replied.

'And don't forget to do Julie.'

Des laughed out loud at my unintended double entendre.

'To do Julie,' he repeated, mimicking my London accent.

He swigged again at his beer and finished it off.

'But first,' he said, as he signalled for more alcohol, 'a little background material.'

* * *

Des Hurrion was born on 23rd July 1956, in Paddington, London.

His mother, Mary, was a Catholic Irish girl who crossed the Irish Sea in the early fifties and found work in London as a chambermaid.

She met a young engineer who persuaded her to do that which she shouldn't, and Mary fell pregnant. The father disappeared, last heard of living in Shepherd's Bush.

The mother was broken by anguish. Her religion was strict and unforgiving on such matters. Having babies out of wedlock was a mortal sin. Now, hell itself beckoned.

'The plan was to have me adopted the minute I arrived,' Des said. 'So she went to a mother and baby home in Highgate and I was born.'

As is always the way in these matters, Highgate is less than a mile away from where I now live.

When Des appeared, the inevitable occurred; the mother's maternal instincts reared up, completely consumed her. Suddenly, she could not abandon her baby son.

A new plan was required to keep her in Des's life.

'She had me fostered to a family in Addlestone, Surrey,' Des said.

'Meanwhile, she tried to find a job as a housekeeper – she was a very good cook – and once she had done that she thought she would then take me back and bring me up in the house she was working in. I was taken to this foster family just before my first Christmas.'

He paused, reached for his beer.

'You know, I have never spent Christmas with my real mum.'

I asked Des if he at least knew the nationality of his father?

'I first heard about my father when I was fifteen,' he explained. 'If you remember I had a talent for playing the piano and my social worker wondered where that talent had come from, so on her own initiative she found out about my father.

'She visited me at Burbank one day with a document and reading it she said she had found out that my father was an engineer.

'She said the document had more information about him and some information about my birth mother; I told her I didn't want to know.

'Subsequently,' he continued, 'I traced my birth mother. During that process I learned four things about my father: he was Irish, he was twenty-eight when I was conceived, he lived in Shepherd's Bush, his name was Ben Kavanagh and he did a runner as soon as he found out my mother was pregnant.'

I had never met my father either, I told Des, and I believed I never would.

'How come?' he asked.

When my mother fell pregnant with me, she was a long-term patient in a Surrey hospital. Naturally, her condition created a huge scandal.

Urgent questions had to be raised. How had this happened? Who was the father? A doctor, heaven forbid? A nurse, heaven forbid? A patient? A groundsman? An outsider?

Whoever it was, a cover up was required, a cover up that existed to this day.

Moreover, my mother never gave up his name, either to the authorities or, later to me.

Two days after my birth I was placed in care and then fostered.

Des too was fostered but his experience had been different to mine. His foster parents adored him. Mine made my childhood a living hell. Des's people sought to give him a kind of loving. Mine cruelly berated me all day long.

Such is the turning of the cards.

Des's foster dad was a glazier by trade and the mum stayed at home.

They had two daughters of their own but they were giving, loving people who were moved to foster abandoned children. Des was later to become their fourth adoption.

'I think my saving grace – my sanity – is that I was really loved in those early years by my adopted parents and by my real mother who came and visited at least once a fortnight,' Des said.

Ironically, a battle between Des's two mothers, his real mum and his foster mum, started to take shape. The battle for Des's heart lasted for two years. Then Mary, Des's birth mother, found work as a steward on a boat sailing round the world.

It was there that Mary met a young man whose entices she could not resist. She fell pregnant again.

The father now gave Mary a cold choice. Either come to America with me, or raise Des and the new baby on your own.

One or the other.

Mary acquiesced to her lover. She chose him over her son. On a day he would never forget, Mary visited Des and told him that she would not see him anymore.

She was starting up a new life and he would not be in it.

This day, this very day, was the last time they would ever see each other.

Des was just three-and-a-half years old.

'I remember it so well,' Des said. 'She told me she was going to America, which is a very stupid thing to say to a three-and-a-half-year-old because America might as well be Isleworth. And then she just walked.'

As she walked away, Des instinctively turned to his foster parents, his safety net. He believed they would catch him and hug him and tell him everything was going to be alright. That the world still existed and he still had a place in it, an important place. But he was wrong.

They did not reach out to him. They did not cuddle him, or embrace him. They too, like Des, stood frosted in confusion.

The effect of their inaction would haunt Des in the most terrible way.

'My foster parents were good people,' Des said, 'but they had been born in the 1900s and they didn't know how to show emotion or affection. I wasn't allowed to show any anger or frustration. What was worse is that when my real mum took me out as a kid, she would say, we'll be together one day and it will all be wonderful. She built up this fairy story which I subliminally took in.

'When she walked out on me that day the fairy story was gone and suddenly I was in harsh reality. She created a fantasy world we were going to be in. Then she left me and that world was gone.'

To deal with the loss, the pain, the confusion, Des reached for every child's first line of defence – fantasy. Every day, he imagined his mum returning to rescue him and taking him off to a lovely house and there he would find laughter and smiles and sunshine days and happy ever afters.

He kept this picture alive his whole childhood.

He had to, otherwise he was dead.

You and I both, I told him.

The years passed. Financially, they were difficult. The sharp edges of poverty started closing in on the family. In all aspects of his life, from food to clothing, there was want.

'I used to have to wear my sister's blouse to school,' he said, 'and of course they button up the wrong way to the boys. I used to get so paranoid that someone would notice. I had to wear her shoes. My feet are knackered now because the shoes were too tight for me.'

At school, Des did not shine. His grades were continually low. He also failed his eleven plus. Not hard to see why. Motherless children rarely prosper academically. Other things on their mind, you see.

Yet Des was lucky. Unlike me, he had a great aptitude for learning music. At home, he played piano, played it extremely well.

Often, when he practised, though, his dad ordered him to play quieter. A streak of anger would then rise in Des and he found himself silently wishing his father would die.

'Unfortunately,' Des said, 'I got my wish.'

In May 1969, his adoptive father contracted emphysema and took to his bed. Des was scheduled to go on a week's holiday at a scout camp. The day before Des's departure, his dad called for him.

'My dad was a fun loving man,' Des said, 'but when he got the illness he became a real curmudgeon. So I walked into the downstairs room and I thought, oh God, here we go again. But when I walked in he was all smiles. He gave me a ten bob note or a pound – I can't remember – but he did it because I was off to scout camp. I couldn't believe it. So I went off to scout camp.

'When I got back my adopted brother ran out of the house and said, "Dad's dead." I remember my foster mother hugging me, which was something she never did, and it being really quite uncomfortable. I didn't like that at all. We were poor then but now we were even poorer.'

His father's death was merely the prelude to the darkened storm heading his way.

Not long after burying the father, the foster mother's granddaughter was diagnosed with flu. Doctors heavily counselled the foster mother against any contact due to her anaemic illness.

The foster mother ignored their warnings. Blood will protect me, she reasoned. She reasoned wrong.

In February 1970, the foster mother was rushed into hospital with major flu symptoms, complicated by her weak immune system.

In her absence, Des, not yet fourteen, was now forced to take on responsibility, become the head of the house.

He cooked, he washed, he cleaned. He made sure his siblings got to and from school, made sure they got to bed on time. He also organised weekly hospital visits where the mother would issue instructions.

Two months into this new life, a policeman knocked on their front door.

'Are you Des Hurrion?' he asked.

'Yes.'

The policeman shifted his feet, looked awkwardly at Des. Then, he spoke.

'I am very sorry to tell you this but your mother has died. Can I come in?'

But Des said, 'No, you can't come in,' and then he remembered himself and added, 'Don't worry. I'll be fine.'

Des closed the door. The first thought that struck him was about their three dogs: now mother had passed, would they be able to survive? That question really bothered him.

'My younger brother broke into tears when he was told,' Des said. 'But I didn't feel anything. I was numb. I had just lost four parents in ten years.'

Social workers were called. Whilst they began assessing the situation, Des stayed at the family house, still cooking, still cleaning, still protecting his siblings.

Then, he was asked to attend an appointment at a solicitor's office. At that meeting, his mum's will was read out.

In it, a major surprise.

His foster mother had ordered that a part of money from the sale of the house would pay for a private education for Des. He would be schooled in an exclusive boarding school. His adoptive mother had reached out from beyond the grave and set him on a new path.

Des was shown a list of prospective boarding schools. He picked a school in Nottingham. He did so because it was the furthest away from the nightmare he now knew as home. He started in September.

Meanwhile, there was summer to negotiate. At first the authorities tried to place Des with his foster family's relations. But those relatives cared not for the golden child.

'I was sent to relatives who didn't really want me,' Des said. 'There was one auntie and uncle in Selsey Bill. The uncle used to smoke all the time, ash falling on his chest. They didn't want me around so I was put into care where I was specifically told I could at least spend holidays with my foster brothers and sisters.'

* * *

Not for him the stability of living in one Home. Instead, Des was moved from one children's home to another without rhyme or reason. He was not allowed to settle but made to move round the country seeking shelter.

'I'd be put in a home and then a bit later I would get a letter from the authorities,' he said. 'It would contain a rail ticket and say, be at this station at this time where so and so is going to meet you. Off I'd go. Then once in that home I'd get another letter.

'Be at this station at this time and so and so will pick you up. I'm thirteen years old with a little blue suitcase going from station to station. I went to Sussex, I went to Norfolk, all over the country. Can you imagine that today?'

Funny word, care, when applied to Des.

The first children's home Des entered was in Hindhead, Surrey.

He arrived on a Friday, the weather absolutely glorious.

It was morning and the Home was deserted. All the kids were on holiday. Des was taken in, sat at a table and given some breakfast. After he finished eating, the woman in charge told him to take a stroll around the grounds so he could become familiar with his new surroundings.

Des walked into the gardens, began exploring. Next thing he knew he had stumbled upon a beauty spot, known locally as the Golden Valley. There he stopped and gazed into its tranquil, breath-taking scenery.

And then it happened, the Orphan's Epiphany arrived and made itself real to him. He was not alone in experiencing its terrible gifts.

All of us who have been abandoned have experienced the moment when we suddenly realise with a deep horror that we are completely and utterly alone in this world: that there is no one to guide us and protect us or help us. There is no mother, no father, no love. The only people on our side are ourselves and we will never be the same again.

All this revealed to Des on the most glorious of summer days.

'I stood on this spot looking down the valley on this beautiful day and I am thirteen years old,' Des said, 'and I said to myself, You are on your own. There is no one there. You are alone but you know what? Part of me was okay about it. Part of me was absolutely terrified and sad. Yet I also felt kind of a thrill because now I was in charge of my own destiny.'

I told Des that my Orphan's Epiphany occurred when I was seven years old. My foster mother had just beaten me with a cane and sent me to bed. The rain was heavy that night, the wind so strong it made the tree outside tap irregularly on my window, creating a sound so menacing, as if the Devil himself was trying to get into my room.

That was the moment which told me I had no one to turn to in life, no one at all.

Most people were given this message – all humans are alone – when death approached. We orphans were given it at a very young age.

I don't know which of us was better off knowing such things. I have always suspected it is us.

Des realised that he had a huge problem. He was a sensitive kid who loved books and played the piano. He suspected that many kids in care did not share such enthusiasms.

In the rough and tumble of a children's home environment, Des knew he would be swallowed up unless he made drastic changes.

In a flash, the answer appeared. He would kill himself, and then create a new Des, develop a new character who was charming and funny and could talk himself out of any situation.

Charm and humour would be his protection from the fists of the unhappy. To achieve this aim, Des had to rid himself of his melancholia, the sadness which shone unmistakeably from his eyes, the sadness which made him an immediate target.

To do so, he took his deep painful emotions and memories and buried them as deep as he could. If they came to mind, he shushed them away, like you did a troublesome pet. It was hard at first but soon he became competent.

And the effect was astonishing.

Within a month, Des Hurrion had become a bright and breezy boy, forever quick with a joke and a smile. Suddenly, everywhere he went, people marvelled at him, wanted to know him. He was irresistible. He told them jokes and they laughed. He was cheeky, irreverent and they patted him on the back.

'I had re-invented myself,' he said. 'For the first time in my life I felt special. It was great, a really good time. Discovering you have ability when everybody has written you off was great. I kind of felt there wasn't much I couldn't do. I had come out of this oppressive environment and suddenly I could express myself, do the things I wanted to do. It was a great time.'

The magic had worked. Beautifully.

People wanted to know Des Hurrion and be with him and I was no exception.

Des arrived at Burbank in the summer of 1970. Another impersonal letter had arrived, containing a rail ticket and orders to be at Woking train station at six in the evening on a certain Sunday.

A Barry Isleworth will pick you up, the letter said.

Des packed his little blue suitcase and trundled off to see where life was now going to take him.

He waited an hour for Barry at Woking train station.

When he finally turned up in his purple Morris Minor, they both realised that they had been waiting for each other at the wrong entrances.

On the way back to Burbank, Des blithely said to Barry, 'I won't be here long. I'm back at school in Nottingham soon and then I'll probably spend the holidays with my little brothers and sisters.'

Barry turned to Des, a little confused.

'Hasn't anyone told you?' he asked.

'Told me what?'

'Your family do not want you to spend time with them. They don't want you. I am sorry. You'll be here at the Home full time now. This is where you now live.'

Ice snagged his stomach, turned his body numb. Bewilderment suffused him. After all he had done for them, his foster family had turned against him, cruelly rejected him.

He arrived at Burbank in a state of shock but as he got out of the car, he suddenly remembered what to do. He reached for his new character. The new Des cracked a smile, buried the hurt and walked into Burbank.

At this point, I had been at Burbank for two years. Even so, I can't recall how Des and I met, what was said, how we bonded; all I know is that very soon after his arrival, Des and I were firm buddies.

Like everyone else, I was mesmerised by him. I wanted his magic. I wanted to be as confident as him, that self-assured. I wanted to play guitar beautifully, write lengthy interesting essays, crack witty remarks, time and time again. Just like Des did.

The only problem I had with Des was that he went away to his boarding school and there was no one else at the Home to fill his shoes. Actually, there was Colin Nollie who I bonded with over music, but his dad took him away after a few months and I never saw him again.

The other kids at the Home I got on with fine. But none were as magical as my Boy Wonder.

During his holidays we hung together as one. He played me Steely Dan records; I played him Bowie and The Faces. We read similar books, swapped authors, gave each other knowledge. We played football in the garden for hours and hours, and then smoked ciggies and tried to kiss the girls. We laughed at staff members, broke rules, and took as much advantage as we could. We grew up together.

And then suddenly I was fifteen, he was seventeen and life was about to change.

* * *

Julie, the head of the house, became a hippie. It seemed the right thing to do. Although a child of the sixties, she had missed out on that decade's massive cultural changes. I did not know why. I suspected she had been too busy obeying everyone – parents, husband, her career – to take part.

Now it was time to time to change all that.

The catalyst for this dramatic change was Julie's husband, Barry Isleworth. Together, they were charged with the running of the Home. I suppose you could say they were the closest any of us would get to a proper mother and a father figure.

At first, their work reflected their marriage: Julie was in charge of staff rotas, the washing of clothes, the feeding of the children. Barry was the boss. He chaired meetings, roared off into town when he felt like it, drank a lot, maintained his own little office, acted the boisterous father figure.

Man first, woman last. It was the early seventies and feminism was a new concept, ripe for mocking. You want to burn your bra, darling? You can guess the rest of the 'joke.'

Whilst she loved him, Julie ignored the unfair balance of their relationship. Love will do that to humans. But when the cracks appeared in the marriage, exacerbated by Barry's drinking and his roving eye, Julie determined to take action.

As her home was bound up in her job, she had nowhere to hide, nowhere to run. She would have to stay, see out the marriage.

That's when she decided to become a hippie. What a great act of revenge, to turn yourself into something your boozy, narrow minded husband would never understand in a million years.

Obviously, Julie would need a crash course in her new chosen subject.

She needed to know her Dylans from her Lightfoots, her Woodstocks from her Isle of Wights, her Hesse from her Kerouac, her kaftans from her afghans.

There was only one man suitable for the job – my fellow orphan and very best friend, Des Hurrion.

Des's obsession with music was as fierce as mine. It began the day a social worker gave him the album, *Fire and Water* by the band Free, and it never abated.

All it took was two plays of that album and down came the posters of his favourite footballers, Manchester City's Franny Lee and Colin Bell, and up went posters of the two main Free men, Paul Rodgers and Paul Kossoff, to take their place.

Des now dressed accordingly. I see him now, sitting in the Home's front room, wearing his blue cheese-cloth shirt, his dark luxurious hair dropping onto his shoulders, playing Free songs on his acoustic guitar, a rock star in aspic.

Julie started gravitating towards Des, started spending a lot of time in his company. I would often find her with Des in the sitting room, her sitting in a chair, sewing, Des playing his guitar or playing records.

Sometimes, he would point out a particular part in a record or tell some story about the band they were listening to, and Julie would instantly stop what she was doing, and lean forward and listen so attentively.

Or maybe he would drop a joke and she would laugh and shake her head in quiet amusement. Oh Desmond.

At first I found this scenario kind of funny. It amused me to hear this woman I thought of as so square, suddenly start talking about Alan Hull's new solo album, *Pipedream*, or what she thought of Hendrix at Woodstock.

Des saw her differently, though.

Julie was not a mother figure to him. She was a bright, attractive woman who paid him loads of attention. He liked that. He liked the new Julie, the one who was opening up day by day, turning into something totally unexpected.

'I remember coming home from working in a part-time job I had,' Des said, 'and everybody had already eaten and Julie saying to me, what would you like to eat? I said, I really fancy fish chips and beans and she went out and cooked it for me. She presented it to me in the dining room and then sat and asked me all about my day. It was kind of weird.'

One night, the inevitable happened in the small corridor that leads from the hall to the kitchen. I can see it now, Des coming one way, Julie towards him.

'She was smiling benignly all over her face,' Des recalled, 'and as we squeezed past she kissed me on the lips. It wasn't a passionate kiss but it was a kiss and it totally freaked me out. I had no idea what was going on. I really don't know what happened but soon she was coming to see me and we were being really naughty. It really is as simple as that.

'There were no women around who fancied me and I was flattered. I was seventeen years old, and wanted a woman to find me attractive. The fact that she was twice my age didn't seem to matter, she was a woman who found me attractive.

'Any woman who made an advance at me at this time was in. I just went with the flow, as I have done all my life. I just did it. I didn't know what was going on, I just knew I enjoyed the attention of this woman and I knew that I liked this woman.

'I always know quickly the people I am going to like and when she changed and became a bit more open, I realised I liked her.'

The affair lasted seven months and was conducted in complete secrecy. That meant deceiving me, four live-in staff, six ancillary workers, twenty children and a husband of seven years standing. A salut, you two.

That was some going.

At first, I suspected nothing. In fact, the idea never crossed my mind and if it had done I would have dismissed it as absolutely preposterous. A member of staff did not sleep with a child. That thought had not even been formed in our collective consciousness. At Burbank, the unacknowledged demarcations were clear. It was kids here, staff over there and never the two shall be at one.

Moreover, Barry, Julie's husband, was not a man you would want to mess around with. This was a beefy man, a capricious man, capable of great and deep anger at the most unpredictable of times.

Then I started growing suspicious.

Des would make the odd remark or disappear and then not be able to satisfactorily tell me where he had been. I noticed that we rarely spent time alone; Julie always seemed to be around.

Finally, on holiday in the Isle of Wight, the truth was revealed. I was on the beach and went to get an ice cream from the kiosk. Next to it was a postcard stand. I wandered over to look at them.

The next thing I knew, I heard Des and Julie talking on the other side of the stand. They thought they were alone.

She was telling him they had to be careful, she thought Barry was getting dangerously suspicious, Des was telling her not to worry. Then they moved off. I gazed at a postcard for two minutes.

Later that day, in a quiet place and moment, I told Des I knew.

'Really,' he said.

'Really,' I replied.

'Ah,' he said.

And then he brought me into his confidence. He told me how he had been seeing Julie for a few months now, how she was desperately unhappy, how her marriage was dead and that they both brought each other happiness.

What I didn't know was that the fires were already cooling. About a month after my discovery, Des and Julie finished.

Why, I asked him thirty-four years after the event?

'Because I had just enrolled at Guildford Technical College and had begun hanging out with girls and boys of my own age. I found it embarrassing to be the lover of a thirty-five-year-old woman,' he coolly said. 'So I ended it.'

In the Home, of course, the relationship was wonderful. It was illicit, exciting. Sneaking down midnight corridors, opening doors slowly, hoping they wouldn't creak, entering a bed for sex with a woman so much older than yourself.

Fantastic. What could be better for a rampant seventeen-year-old?

But at college, amongst his own age, his own kind, the attraction waned.

There was another reason for Des breaking away from Julie.

Rock 'n' roll. May sound silly but you have to understand that for Des music was the most important thing in the world to him. Why? Because music was the creator of his dreams, the father of his visions. Music shaped a world inside his mind's eye and Des went to live there.

'One of things that my 1970s rock and roll did was to romanticise the itinerant,' Des said.

'Listen to the song, *I'm A Mover* by Free. There is a line about being born by a river and like that river, the guy has been moving since. Can I associate myself with that? Damn right, I can. You're talking about someone who had been shunted around for five years. And check out the lyrics to a John Miles song called *Remember Yesterday*.

'There is a line that says something about how he has been everywhere but still has no place to go. What better way to deal with a peripatetic life than to realise it was actually quite cool? Rock 'n' roll music really did change my life. Suddenly there is this wonderful world you can go into with these sounds and lyrics.'

I knew this escape route well. In fact, I knew it back to front. Music gave me hours of welcome escape, took me off to faraway worlds, fantastic places. Yet Des took things much further than me.

Some months into his course, he quit further education for good. He hopped on a boat to France where he busked and made his living.

Des and his guitar, and the open road. Told you he was braver than me. I'd never have made such a move. Fear would have stopped me. The world still scared me at this point.

'I left college because I wanted to be free of institutions,' he said. 'The boarding school, the Home, college... Also my work was suffering because of this liberated rock 'n' roll lifestyle I was living and there were no adults to tell me what a stupid decision I was making, although my course tutor tried.'

Des returned to Britain, got a job, got a flat.

'I did what most people do at that age,' he said, 'which is listen to rock 'n' roll music, drink too much and just have the time of my life.'

In 1977, he went with friends to the Guildford Civic Hall to see a band called Thin Lizzy. Who should be standing in the bar when he arrived? Julie. They got talking.

Telephone numbers were swapped.

Julie had now left Barry, had her own place where she lived with her daughter, Susan.

Soon, the inevitable. The pair were re-united. Des went to live with Julie. But it would never work. Des had left college to pursue the magic that can free your soul. Instead, he found himself with a job, a wife, a child.

'It wasn't where I wanted to be,' Des stated. 'I wanted to live in London and I didn't care where it was.'

I too needed London to save me but Des took a different route to Our Blessed City of Salvation, the city that allows you to re-invent yourself, re-make yourself, to do as Des had done, and forget all. London breathes its past on all its citizens but its future is what excites, what allows us to hide our pasts.

One morning, Des opened up a map of London, shut his eyes and placed his finger on the page.

He opened his eyes. His finger was placed in the middle of the Thames River. No good. He repeated the action. His finger hit Watford. Elton John territory. Not good.

'The third place I hit was a place called Gunnersbury which is West London, Chiswick,' he said.

'I took the day off sick and I went to Gunnersbury to have a look around. There is nothing at Gunnersbury. There is the

Brentford flyover and a roller disco which tells you how long ago it was. I went back and looked at the map and saw that Ealing was near Gunnersbury and Ealing resonated. I suppose because I had heard of Ealing Broadway, Ealing Common, Ealing Studios. I thought okay, I'll live in Ealing.'

One day, the inevitable happened. Des and Julie got into a massive row. Shortly afterwards, he packed his bags.

He travelled to Ealing Broadway station, and then asked a cab driver to take him to the cheapest hotel. Two weeks later he applied for a job as a barman at a local pub.

'I had to start all over again. No friends, didn't know anybody. Got a job in a local pub after two weeks. Went into the pub on Thursday and the landlord told me you are working tomorrow night with a guy called Chris.

'That night, this bloke walked in at eight o'clock and said, "Hi, I'm Chris." We worked the shift and had a good laugh, and at the end I said, "Do you fancy a pint one night?" He said, "Yeah all right," and like all the key relationships in my life I knew straight away that I was going to know him forever.'

The very next night he met a woman called Margie and a man called Wig. To this day, all three have been his closest friends. Like me, like so many other orphans I suspect, his friends became his family.

Soon after, Des left the pub, moved on. He took on casual jobs, worked as a postman, a fork-lift driver before deciding to get serious and take a computer course.

Naturally, he passed. He began working in IT, working his way up to manager status. But something was not quite right.

* * *

Every now and then, especially after a weekend of heavy drinking, he would suffer panic attacks.

He put these attacks down to his large alcohol intake. But one day at work, a Monday, he went to the pub at lunchtime for the boss's birthday drink.

At one point, feeling a little giddy, he went to the toilet.

And it was there that Des Hurrion fell to pieces.

He recalled, to me, strange, frightening sensations that rushed through his body. He remembered how fear filled up his stomach quicker than booze ever did. He recalled how he rushed out of that toilet shaking, and afraid to his very soul, as if death had just brushed by his shouder.

'I walked over Putney Bridge. I thought I was having a heart attack,' Des said. 'It was a nightmare. The next day this depression moved in, this dreadful depression. It was like carrying a cow on my shoulders. I remember walking round the park and I could feel this thing on me, on my shoulders, on my head.

'I really needed a break but I had to work, I had to pay the rent so every day I dragged myself into work. A lot of people at that time described me as looking shell shocked. And they were right, I was finally diagnosed with post-traumatic stress disorder. I must have looked awful every morning coming into work. I stuck it out for a couple of years and then I went into counselling.'

Luckily, Des happened upon a sympathetic psychiatrist. As their sessions lengthened, enlightenment slowly dawned. Answers appeared.

He was shown that the character he had created to protect himself with had fallen apart. All the hurt that he had pushed downwards had now surfaced. That was why the pain was so unrelenting. That was why the black despair gripped so tightly.

They went back further and further and further until they came upon that dreadful day, the day when Des's mother walked away from him, and so, in their unwitting way, did his foster parents.

'I had locked it away but it wouldn't stay locked,' Des quietly said.

'The simple fact is that at the age of three-and-a-half I had my heart broken and wasn't allowed to express the pain and the anger and the fear that I felt.

'My social worker once brought up the subject of my mother and I remember very clearly being very practical and saying, "Oh it's fine, she's got her thing to do." But I couldn't deal with it and my brain imploded. So I had a dreadful time for a very long time. From my late twenties to my early forties, in fact.'

As children, we had no understanding of adults. If they hit us, we became convinced it was our fault. We knew not their motives. How could we? We could hardly stand on our own two feet.

When I discovered in later life that my foster mother had experienced a bad childhood, a heavy load was instantly lifted off me. I now knew I was not bad or stupid, or any of those other terrible names she had spat out at me. The pain she was in had caused her to lash out. I just happened to be in the way. Unfortunate. Unlucky. Terrible. But you know what?

Knowing that I was not to blame gave me a tremendous kick-start.

At thirty-nine years of age, Des decided to track down his real mother. He needed to confront her. He needed understanding. He needed her to heal him.

At first, he thought she was in America but he was wrong. After a year of hunting he was astonished to find that one of her recent addresses was just two miles away from where he lived. They had probably passed each other by in the street and never realised it.

He discovered that she had married the father of her second child and had had two more children with him. The man had then run (as they do) and she had raised the family on her own. Then she went back to Ireland. Des found her address and sent her a letter.

'I said in the letter that I didn't want to upset her life but just wondered how she was and who she was,' Des said, his voice now slowing. This is such hard territory for him to enter.

'She phoned me. She is thirty years older than me and she sounded like an old woman. It was such a shock because I remember when she was young. We had a brief talk and at the end of it she said, "I love you Desmond," and I said, "I love you very much, Mum."'

This was the first time mother and son had told each other that. Des was in his late thirties at the time.

The phone calls continued but when Des suggested a meeting, she shocked Des. She said no.

The stigma of illegitimacy still frightened her. 'She thought, if someone found out that she had a son, she would lose her friends, lose her kids, and that she would be vilified all these years later for having a child out of wedlock,' Des explained.

'She couldn't cope with it at all. So we had a phone call relationship. We did plan to meet but she let me down a couple of times. It was a very painful eight or nine months. She sent me a jumper for my fortieth birthday and a card with a car on the front like a kid's card, which was weird. She also sent me a couple of photographs of her. I had never seen anyone who looked like me before. We were two peas in a pod. I could have been her brother.'

Des Hurrion retained just one happy instant from this time. Speaking to her on Hallowe'en, his mum said, 'You know I don't believe in witches.'

To which her son replied, 'You haven't seen some of the women I've been out with.'

Both mother and son laughed out loud together. They had never done that before. It felt good.

'But it wasn't going anywhere,' Des continued. 'I phoned her in February of 1996 and she was in a foul mood on the phone. She accused me of having people spy on her in Ireland. She was really paranoid.

'I phoned her back and said, look this is not healthy; don't call me back and I won't call you. Then I put the phone down.'

Yet she still haunted him, still exerted a massive pull on his soul. How could she not? She was his mother.

A year later, Des wrote again to her. In the letter, he told her not to respond, that there was no point staying in touch, but he wanted to tell her one thing, and that was this – I will always love you, O mother of mine.

As he told me this, tears started up in his eyes. Such tragedy. Mother and son, torn apart by religion, by circumstance, unable to help each other, to grow, to live as intended, in happiness, in love. I felt helpless.

Des wiped his eyes, moved his head left and right, attempted to shake himself clear of the sadness gripping him.

Another swig of beer, then he started up again, his tone more measured, more matter of fact.

'I was very pissed off over Easter and I couldn't understand why,' he said.

'Then I realised it was the ninth anniversary of me getting in touch with her. I wrote myself a note which said, I am free. That was three months ago and that's when it ended.

'I do understand and I forgive. Because when she left me she had my sister Alex inside her and she made the right decision. She had an unborn baby and she was with a guy that she thought would be okay. I don't have a problem with that, I just have a problem with all the pain it has caused me.'

He paused. 'I always feel that all my life I have been tidying up someone else's mess. But the thing is I have come to terms with it all. I understand about my mother, I have recovered from the breakdown and to be honest, I like my life now.'

The clock struck ten.

I looked down and saw that the ashes of the words we had spoken were piled up around our feet. Empty beer bottles stood close to white plates which were smeared with dark sauce and coloured foods.

For a brief second or so, the walls of the Chinese restaurant faded in and out, in and out, out and in. Alcohol was once more threatening to take me on a long holiday from myself.

The bill arrived, money was exchanged.

Des walked me to the station in the black cold country night and we hugged goodbye.

On the train home, I thought of Des living alone at forty-nine years of age, not married, childless. For most people this would be the tragedy. Life is about children, about togetherness.

Yet there are other routes to take in life and just as meaningful. Who is to argue differently?

As Bill S. once wrote, to thine ownself be true.

All in all, I thought Des happy. After all, he had his freedom, the precious freedom that music showed him as a kid and still means so much to him today.

Music made him unfettered, unafraid. God bless music. Today, Des Hurrion has the ability to go with the flow of his life, to go wherever his soul dictates, see where it takes him, whether that be as an IT manager in charge of an office, in charge of people, or as a barman in an Ealing pub full of drama.

It is the same freedom he exuded at the Home. My man still believed in the magic that can change your soul. It made me so happy.

A week later, I wrote an e-mail to Des.

From: paolo@gmail.com

To: desh@hotmail.com

Subject: The New Book

Des – Hope all well, amico. Finished writing your chapter last night and have attached it above. I was hoping you could take a look at it, correct any mistakes, dates, etc. The first thing that struck me was how similar our starts in life had been. Both our mothers were Catholic immigrants who escaped to England from highly religious and restrictive societies. Both of them carried such high hopes for their future and both tragically floundered.

Unintentionally, they brought two boys into this world whose lives would be heavily touched by pain, misery, extreme difficulty.

The only difference was this: The bulk of my pain occurred in childhood.

Yours, unfortunately, would not let go and savage you again in later life.

I have to say I was really moved by a lot of what you had to say. That image of you as a small child with your little blue suitcase being shunted from home to home is one that will stay with me a very long time. I really think it a damning indictment of how badly valued children (especially motherless ones) were in this country. I use the past tense. I can only write what I see but I think there has been a positive sea shift in child rearing. I just look at my friends who are fathers and they are fantastically involved with their children, probably in ways that their fathers had not been.

They really have placed themselves at the centre of their kid's lives, have fully accepted commitment and responsibility. I really do admire them for those qualities. And in the world of care I see positive changes. Since *The Looked After Kid* was published I have been invited to many care functions and conferences to give readings. I normally do a reading of ten mins, take questions and then afterwards speak to social workers, foster parents, etc.

Everyone I meet seems genuinely anxious to do their very best for kids in care.

I did a reading at a home in Birmingham once. Never forget it. I read the opening chapter where I talk about the bedroom that the eight of us shared, the crappy clothes we had to wear, the lack of money, the lack of everything really. When I finished there was a silence and then this girl exclaims, 'Man, you're old school!'

Turns out they all had their own rooms, forty pounds a week pocket money, and could basically come and go as they pleased.

I used to think I was like the great Spurs footballer Jimmy Greaves and could perfectly time my runs into the penalty area of life and score with ease. Going by what those kids told me, I am wrong. I think we both landed in care about twenty years too early. Being facetious. Of course, all those kids, forty quid a week or not, will suffer the same problems and experiences we did. Money and riches won't change that. You have to go inwards, stage a revolution of your mind and heart, to beat that which would bring you to your knees.

Better go. *The Sopranos* are on TV in a minute. You should watch it. Best show ever. Get in touch after you have read the chapter. Also am going to see Norman Bass next week. He lives down near Brighton. Best ones, Paolo

Two

The Runaway Boy

The Story of Norman Bass

Let us pray.

At five years of age, I loved going to mass. My vindictive foster mother was not Catholic so, on blessed Sunday mornings, I was given an hour and a half out of her company. I could not have been happier.

Mass was my safe haven from her, a place of ritual and forgiveness, of incense and kindly priests, and songs with fine melodies, stirring choruses. God held out the promise of love and heaven. Every day, I ached for His blessed deliverance from my dark world.

Nothing bad happened to me in that church and that's why I loved it so. Not long after my first mass I became an altar boy. At first I stood at the altar holding a giant candle. It made me feel grown up.

Then I graduated to passing Father Tucker the communion cup. I liked Father Tucker a lot. He was a good man, the kind of man you want a priest to be, so warm, so approachable, so kindly.

One Sunday, Father Tucker gathered us altar boys together, told us that a special mass would be held that week to celebrate the moment when Jesus washed the feet of his disciples.

Twelve men from the congregation had already volunteered to take part in the ceremony. However, Father Tucker cautioned, in case someone failed to show, he would call upon one of us altar boys to make up the number whose feet he would wash. Be ready was his message.

He then asked us to come to church on the Wednesday morning for a rehearsal.

I duly attended the run through and then went home. I spent the afternoon alone, kicking a ball in a light rain that sprinkled diamonds on the garden. That evening I went to church expecting a huge attendance. When I walked in I saw that most of the pews were empty. Most of the volunteers had stayed at home. Mass went ahead.

When the part of the mass that required the washing of the feet arrived, Father Tucker had no choice. He gestured for every altar boy present to come forward.

I sat on the bench and took off my shoes. In a line of gleaming white feet, mine stood out unforgivably. They were caked in about an inch of mud. Playing football on a rainy afternoon will do that for you.

When Father Tucker reached me I saw a look of great holy disdain cross his face. He hastily dabbed my feet with his towel and then moved off. Worse was to follow.

In the rehearsal that morning I had not really paid much attention to Father Tucker's instructions. As usual, my mind was in the clouds and my feet walked in other worlds.

My negligence would now come back to haunt me.

At one point in the service we had to leave the altar, kneel in front of a statue of the Virgin Mary, and pray.

I was at the back of the group so when we stood and turned, I was the leader. For some reason (those clouds fogging up my brain again), I believed the mass had finished.

So I led everyone back into the vestry.

After a minute or so, one of the boys asked, 'Where's Father Tucker?'

Another boy looked through the curtain. 'Blimey,' he said. 'He is out there on his own. I don't think mass has finished.'

When Father Tucker finally came into the vestry, he made straight for me.

'What were you doing?' he demanded. 'You led everyone away. Didn't you hear my instructions this morning?'

My cheeks flushed violent red; I bowed my head in shame. I had never seen him this angry.

'I don't know,' he said, exasperated. He moved away and addressed all of us.

'For taking part in mass tonight – such as it was,' he said, glancing back at me, 'everyone is to receive a Winston Churchill Crown. These are special coins that will grow in value over the years and therefore are very much worth putting away and saving.'

Although I felt I should refuse the present given my conduct that night, treats in my life were rare. I slipped it into my pocket.

To assuage my guilt, I made a deal with myself. I would keep the coin until I was an adult. And then I would cash it in for huge amounts of money, give some to Father Tucker, and then be rich and safe for ever more. Amen.

When I returned home I made sure to carefully hide the coin from my foster mother. If she discovered it, I would never see it again.

On the day I moved into Burbank, I still possessed that coin. I handed it to Barry Isleworth, the head of the Home, with great care and watched as he placed it in the petty cash tin which was kept in his little office by the front door.

When I turned eighteen and left Burbank, I asked for my coin. A staff member went to retrieve it but could not find it anywhere. After much thought and deliberation, we realised what had happened.

Many years back the petty cash tin had been stolen. My Churchill coin was in the tin. I was stupefied. A potential fortune had been stolen from me.

'What child stole it?' I asked.

No one could remember.

Thirty years later I discovered the thief's identity. His name is Norman Bass.

And this is his story.

* * *

He sat in the police station, alone. It was two in the morning and he wondered how it was that every time he ran away, the police kept managing to track him down.

I am like a human boomerang, he thought to himself, with a rueful smile. I fling myself as far as I can but somehow or other I always come flying back.

I should join the circus.

A policeman bustled past him and then there was silence again. He was glad no one was talking to him. When you have a stammer as bad as Norman's, you are always glad when people ignore you.

That way you are not forced to watch people trying to hide their smiles or uneasiness at your malady as you try to engage in conversation.

He looked up and saw a series of small posters pinned to a noticeboard.

'If you see a crime, tell us,' one said. Fat chance of that, he thought to himself.

Then he saw another poster, a poster that would inadvertently set in motion dark and terrible things.

The poster in question told Norman Bass, the serial runaway boy, that British citizens could buy a one day passport and travel to France.

He read it and then read it again. A sense of excitement ran through him. Of course, why not? Next time he plans to, he will acquire one of those passports. And go to France.

France. No bugger would catch me there. And better still no one could talk to me. I am English, they are French. I can disappear. Forever.

In France.

Suddenly, Norman Bass's life seemed a lot brighter.

The policeman came back and placed himself in front of him.

'Mr Isleworth has just arrived to take you home, sonny.'

Norman stood up and picked up his small bag. He had already anticipated how Barry would act towards him.

Either he will be loudly shouted at, either in public or in private, or he will be submitted to the silent treatment for a number of weeks.

Actually, Norman thought to himself, I don't care what he does. I have got a plan, now. And no one is going to stop me.

* * *

His wife Tania had thoughtfully made us sandwiches for lunch. They sat in the fridge. She sat at her work.

Norman and Tania lived in a quiet village about thirty minutes out of Brighton. Theirs was a deep relationship. Norman told me that Tania was nothing less than his saviour, an amazing woman whose love and care had healed so many of his wounds.

Love, he revealed, had been the most decisive force in his life.

Norman's house was unprepossessing, not out of the ordinary. Good sized rooms, family photos on the wall, lamps, a certain cosiness. He surprised me when he told me it was rented. I assumed he maintained a mortgage, such was the sense of responsibility he exuded.

It was a good time for us to talk. Yesterday, Norman had organised his stepson's thirteenth birthday. Kristian, Tania's thirteen-year-old son, went paintballing, then had his mates to the house for a barbeque.

Norman had cooked.

At five in the afternoon, Kristian turned to Norman and said, 'Dad, this is the best birthday ever,' and Norman quickly felt tears gather at the back of his eyes.

His emotion was not a surprise to him. As a child, there was not one of his birthdays that he could remember with any fondness. Now he had made another's memorable. It was a rare achievement.

He brought coffee out of the kitchen and we sat at a table.

'Ready when you are,' he said.

I switched on the recorder and pushed it towards him. 'Start at the beginning,' I said.

Norman Bass was born on 17th January 1960 in Thornton Heath in Surrey, not far from Croydon.

His mum worked for the Quaker Oats Porridge people and his dad was a factory worker.

Not long after he was born the family moved to a new council house in Camberley. Everything was going well.

Then it happened – Norman awoke one day with a terrible stammer. No one knew where it came from.

'At first, it was very embarrassing,' he said. 'Then, at primary school, it absolutely consumed me. It terrified me to the point where when the teacher shouted out my name for register, I couldn't even say, "Yes miss."'

Eight o'clock in the morning and already the day had been made bitter and sour, made cruel beyond any repair.

'I started to play truant,' he said, 'simply because that way I wouldn't have to answer the register. I used to forge notes from my mum saying I was ill. Then my brother came along. Soon after that I started to run away from home. The first time I went was at Christmas time.

'I pinched a tin of ham out of the Christmas hamper and my dad's bicycle and I cycled fifty miles to my auntie's house in Oxfordshire. I was ten years old. It took me a day. I literally turned up on her doorstep, stayed overnight, and then Dad came and got me on the train and took me home.'

This overwhelming urge to run was not hard to figure out. On the road, you rarely have to talk to anyone. That's a very big attraction for a kid with a terrible stammer, especially one whose stammer had now started attracting the vindictive attention of the school bullies.

'There was one incident I'll always remember,' Norman said. 'There was this huge kid at school and one day he punched me so hard in the face that he split my nose wide open. I went home crying and the next day my mother took me into school to see the headmistress. Because of my stammer, all I could say to this woman was that this kid had punched me. Her reaction was to poke me in the chest really hard and say I don't have kids in my school, kids are baby goats.'

Norman's parents were accepting people, not ones to complain or assert themselves. They were very English in that way. Norman's parents meekly accepted the headmistress's dismissive behaviour towards their son. And walked away.

'The inability of adults to understand what is being said by the young is both the joy and tragedy of childhood,' I announced.

Norman looked at me quizzically. I had been reading a lot of Oscar Wilde lately, I explained, and his influence hung heavy on me.

Norman raised his eyebrows, continued his story.

'One day,' Norman told me, 'I was so badly beaten by a gang of kids, that to this day I can still remember the savagery of their punches. But when I got home again my parents refused to do anything about it. They said they didn't want to make a fuss and report it to anyone. I remember thinking then, why won't you do this for me?'

Worse, Norman's uncle came to stay at the house. He acted pleasantly. Until Sunday, when Norman's parents would go to church. As soon as they had departed, the uncle turned, began threatening Norman with violence, with severe beatings.

In response, Norman began wetting his bed on a nightly basis. Instead of asking why this had happened, his parents became enraged with their son. They too threatened him with violence.

So he started running away from them on a regular basis.

'My parents' way of dealing with my running away was to bring in these heavyweights from the church to come over and threaten me,' he said, smiling. 'They would threaten me with purgatory and all these things. It didn't stop me. I just ran away again.'

'When I ran away,' he said, 'I never had any idea where I was going. It was always the going rather than the arriving. Anyway, I found myself sitting on Teignmouth seafront one night.

'Then this lad, who couldn't be any older than me, came along and asked me, was I okay? I said I had nowhere to sleep so he took me home to his mum and dad who, of course, phoned the police. Dad came down on the train the next day to get me.

'When I came home I was told a social worker was coming to see me. I had never heard of these people before. The social worker came and she told me, we are going to take you away from home because we think you are beyond parental control. She came back a couple of days later.

'She drove a blue Austin car. I had no idea where I was going or what was going on. All I knew was that I was going into care, whatever the hell that meant.'

I told Norman I knew that sense of confusion well. When they told me I was being put into care, it was as if they were talking a different language.

I knew nothing about children's homes or social workers. The closest I had gotten to the subject at that point was the Charles Dickens novel, *Oliver Twist.*

'I didn't know either,' Norman cheerfully replied. 'The social worker said she was going to take me to this place and I would spend some time there with some very nice people until they worked out what was best for me.

'So they drove me to Guildford. In the car was my mum and this social worker. I remember we turned into this long driveway with this big posh house at the end of it and as we drove up there were children running around in the garden. This was Woodrough.'

'Woodrough? You and I and both,' I said, excitedly.

'So you knew the wonderful John and Molly Brown?'

'Lovely people Molly and John Brown, or Auntie Molly and Uncle John as it was back then,' Norman said. 'John was this little man with curly hair and glasses and a pipe and Molly had on this housecoat. They took me in and they got one of the boys to show me round.

'Then I was taken into this little playroom and I remember standing on this wooden floor and I watched my mum drive down the road. I had been left again. There were tears. I was crying but then Auntie Molly came in and she was great.

'She introduced me to a couple of the kids of my own age and I was shown upstairs to this big bedroom with six or eight beds. It was all very new and a bit scary but they did try to shelter me from the strangeness of it all.'

I too knew the strangeness of it all. Entering care robbed you of your gravity. You went into free fall. Suddenly, everything you knew had gone. Vanished. Nothing was solid, nothing seemed real. No more certainties. You don't know where you are, worse, who you are.

People you had never met before looked after you. Strangers fed you, told you to do jobs, told you when to get dressed, when to sleep, when to eat, when to work, when to play.

You were completely adrift from the life you once knew.

There was the vastness of your new home to comprehend, the big garden, the many bedrooms, the playrooms. You have never seen the like before. You lived in a house built for the rich but now populated by you and your peers, and you were known as the abandoned.

As Norman said, the strangeness of it all.

Worse, the kids there had the edge on you. They knew the rhythm of the Home's life, the rules, the customs. They trumped you and in doing so they created a tangible and dangerous vulnerability in and around you.

You walked uncertainly, you talked carefully, you tried to hold your nerve. You lived, unprotected.

And then suddenly, there was a click, a loud click, and you woke up and found you had landed, found your feet, adapted, worked it out.

Somehow, against your will, you had become a part of this once strange world, become a part of its tapestry. That was the day you officially became an orphan.

'At Woodrough, there was a school with two classrooms in the grounds,' Norman said.

'Yes,' I replied, 'I remember them, but why didn't they send us to a proper school?'

'Don't you know?' Norman asked, somewhat surprised at my question.

'Because they didn't know how long we would be at Woodrough for?' I asked.

'No,' Norman said, 'they had to build them because the headmaster of the local school wouldn't take orphans.'

'What?'

'It is true. The local headmaster wouldn't take us. Didn't want us in his school.'

'But why? Why would this man reject us in such a callous manner?'

Because England was a country built on class, its people judged by blood. Blood fixed your position in English society. Top of the line, the royal family, bottom of the pile, orphans.

That is why many refer to us as having 'bad blood.' We are born bad, we die bad. There is no redemption. We will always be unwanted within their circles.

The headmaster's decision to ban orphans from his school was no doubt based on that calculation. He must have worried that we would not be able to help ourselves from being wild, uncontrollable, disrupting forces, driven in fury by our bad blood.

Yet, stupid as these assumptions of his were (after all, applied to a race of people they would be automatically deemed racist) a kind of understanding for this man grew inside of me.

The headmaster knew nothing of the orphan and how could he? And in fact how could anyone? Our presence in the world was low, minimal.

We had no one to explain us. We lived in mysterious buildings, far away from the view of the community, our homes placed behind fences or large hedges.

The children's home rarely featured in people's lives or communities in the way the school, the church, the sports club, the pub, the bingo hall, the football ground, did. All of these are a part of people's lives.

Children's homes are not. They are invisible, hidden away like a bad secret.

Easy then for myths to be built around them and easy for those myths to have assumed the force of truth. I would venture that most people's idea of the Home is that depicted in *Oliver Twist*, the book and film and I would not blame anyone for thinking in such a manner.

It is precisely how I thought of them until I was placed in one.

'I started running away again,' Norman said. 'I wasn't very adventurous. It was just going up the road or going into Guildford where they would catch me and bring me back. I obviously didn't know where the staff lived so a couple of times I was actually picked up by the staff coming into work.

'In fact I later found out that I had one of the longest records for staying at Woodrough. They couldn't figure out where to send me because they couldn't figure out why I was running away. I was there for about seven months.

'Molly and John were still very good to me. They never put pressure on me to explain my actions. And one of the things I do remember about my time there was the treat of being able to go and spend the evening in the Browns' sitting room. It was a wood panelled room at the end of the house. I remember variety shows on the telly and all of us sat around in our dressing gowns and pyjamas eating chocolate and having a whale of a time. It was great.'

I too had been given the healing treatment from the Browns and it really moved me that nearly forty years after life in their care, two grown men had met and remembered, with full gratitude, the good they gave them. The value of their work resonated to this day and beyond. It was a fantastic achievement by the pair of them.

Norman's parents visited him at Woodrough. He was also allowed home on certain weekends. Even then he couldn't help himself.

'My stammer was still a problem,' he said. 'I had the piss taken out of me relentlessly by the other kids because whenever anyone asked me anything there were these huge pauses. I remember we had to do an IQ test at Woodrough and apparently I came out quite high. But it took me ages to answer their questions.

'Then one day I was told I was moving to this new Home in Woking and it was called Burbank. I was really upset. I had built up this great relationship with the Browns and all the kids.

'I thought, I know I've been naughty but I loved it there. It was so cosy and the Browns were so loving and so supportive.

I disliked running away from there more than anywhere else because I was made to feel wanted at Woodrough.'

I recalled my last day there as well, choking in incomprehension that a child so happy should be removed from the very heart of that joy by the people who professed to care for him. I would not believe that John and Molly Brown no longer cared for me.

Norman had exactly the same thoughts.

'So on this particular day,' Norman said, 'this old Morris Minor estate trundled up the drive and this big beer bellied man with a goatee, all happy and bouncy got out and that was Barry. I remember that John and Molly were stood on the doorstep when I arrived and they were stood on the doorstep when I left.

'Molly was crying and I was crying and Barry bundled me into the car and I remember trying to look back up the drive as the car pulled away and thinking that somewhere on the drive a barrier would suddenly come down and John and Molly would run up and say he can stay! But of course that was never going to happen.'

Exactly my thoughts, I told Norman, excitedly. I really thought that just as we got to the end of the drive, Barry would stop and say, 'Fooled you kid,' and open the passenger door and let me out of the car and then I would run back up the drive and into the arms of the people I adored.

But the car never stopped. It just kept on going. Now I see, that car never stopped.

For any of us.

* * *

Norman thought about that first day at Burbank, the day he placed himself in my orbit.

'We drove to Burbank,' Norman said, 'and again, it was the big drive with the big house and lots of kids in the garden and then into the hallway with those red tiles and I remember thinking, oh well not quite as big as Woodrough but it felt the same.

'Barry took me through to the sitting room and there was Julie and she was very nice. Even so it was all very strange – new kids, new staff, new experience and of course because I was wound up from leaving Woodrough my stammer was really pronounced.

'The first thing Barry did was to start taking the piss out of it. He would shout, in that pseudo Welsh accent of his, "What's the matter with you boy?" I remember thinking hasn't anyone told you?'

I was surprised to hear this of Barry. He was many things Barry – domineering, loud, forceful – but he never struck me as cruel. Perhaps it was his self-defence mechanism, buying time while he figured out what to do with a kid who stammered his every word.

'I was taken upstairs, shown my bedroom. It was just two beds. Then I was taken down to the local school and enrolled there and then I started getting used to this new routine. It must have been just a few weeks but pretty soon I started to run away again. It is hard to explain the motives behind it. I just got this urge. I had to go.

'Sometimes things would trigger it. I remember specifically we were sat in the TV lounge and there was this travel programme on about Canada and it was showing waterfalls and the scenery and the next day I got dressed, pretended to go to school and just buggered off.

'Other times, I would leg it because of my stammer. Barry didn't get the point of how terrified I was of being made a fool of and feeling a fool with this stammer. If I said goodnight to him he would always reply with a g-g-g-g-g-good – n-n-n-night. And then laugh.

'I ran away so many times. One time I went off with one of the girls in the Home. I was having an occasional thing with her, the occasional snog that kind of thing. We ended up deciding to run away together. The only place I could think of to go to was my auntie's in Oxfordshire. I don't know how we got up there, we might have thumbed lifts. We were twelve, thirteen, and it was extremely risky, a boy and girl together like that on the road.'

'The naivety of youth often protects its reckless nature,' I said.

Oscar once more, and Norman, again, nonplussed.

'I remember I nicked a cardboard punnet of mushrooms from the front of a greengrocer,' Norman said. 'That was all we had to eat. Soon, she had had enough, so she went into a shop near where my aunt lived, she went in there and gave herself up.

'I panicked and went into Oxford as fast as I could and got the first train out. You could buy platform tickets then so I just did that and got on the first train and hid in the toilets. By the time I got off the train it was dark and I was in Birmingham New Street. I got back on the train and hid in the toilets again and the train moved off. Turned out it was the Edinburgh sleeper.

'Not sure how they managed it but I got discovered and by the time we got to Edinburgh the transport police were waiting for me. They took me off to this remand home in the middle of Edinburgh. I was absolutely terrified. All these tough kids and me the little Southerner with the stammer.'

I told Norman I understood his fear.

My school once organised a day visit to the local borstal. One resident, tall, imposing, came and stood in front of me.

'I like your shoes,' he said.

'Thank you,' I replied.

'Now fucking take them off and give them to me,' he demanded.

Luckily, a teacher was passing nearby.

Borstal boys were tough. To be locked up with them in Scotland with a stammer and an English accent was probably not the best asset to be defending yourself with.

'I was seen by a few people and then I had to go to their little school where they left me to do drawing,' Norman said. 'I remember everything was in lock down. Go into a corridor it would be locked. Go into the showers and come out, it's locked. I thought it was an awful place.

'Then they told me that a senior member of staff from Burbank was coming up to get me. It was Maggie, her being from Scotland. All the kids, myself included, hated Maggie but she was great to me that time probably because she had got a free weekend out of it. And we flew back. None of this going back on the train malarkey.

'I remember getting off the plane at Heathrow, coming down this escalator and there was Barry standing at the bottom looking up at me with that stern face of his.

'I was almost wetting myself with fear thinking what is he going to say to me? I got to the bottom of the escalators and he just turned around and he walked. We got in the car and he didn't say a word during the drive back home. It was the scare-the-shit-out-of-him-with-the-stony-silence routine. Got in, was sent to bed and told not to speak to anyone about what I had done or where I had been.'

Barry's deepest concern soon became apparent. Had Norman and the girl coupled? Given Barry's obsession with sex I now wonder if his questions did not reflect some form of personal interest.

He was always wolf whistling women from his car as he rushed down Woking High Street, always making lewd remarks. He once told me off when I failed to comment on a bronzed beauty who had just walked by. Of course, it was inappropriate behaviour, the behaviour of a man with a twisted mind, living in a sexless marriage.

What's funny about his questioning of Norman is that his subject had no idea what he was talking about. Sex at that time was a mystery to Norman. He knew kisses, but that was all.

'Barry asked me, "Did you kiss her?" I said yes. Then he lent forward and he said, "Did you do this as well?" And he made a hole with one hand and stuck a finger through it with the other. I thought, I don't know what the fuck you are talking about? What is that? Then it dawned on me and I thought, ah so that's how you do it, that's what that is for. I had just been given the facts of life, thanks Barry.'

Norman's truancy had so far been confined to Great Britain. Inevitably, that had to change. The will to show those charged with his keep how unhappy he was had to assert itself.

He now thought of the one day passport to France offer. At the same time, he made another crucial realisation. His stammer made people think he was stupid. That was fine by him. It gave him the freedom to make all kinds of moves. Of him, no one would suspect anything untoward.

To secure a one day passport to France, he needed money. So the first thing he did was to buy a larger satchel than the one he normally used for school. He carried that bigger satchel for about three weeks. He wanted everyone to get used to seeing him with it. He also obtained a large plastic bag which he hid in the satchel.

Then, one morning, he made his move.

After breakfast, Norman dawdled in the Home's cloakroom. Jimmy and David and Graham and Sarah and Anne, and all the others, were busily putting on their blazers and shoes and adjusting ties and shirt buttons, before leaving for school; a crowd of noise and colour setting sail once more for the local classrooms.

Norman waited patiently for them to go. No one minded him. They rarely did. When the last child had departed, Norman came out of the cloakroom, and walked through the playroom into the hallway. The staff were in the kitchen.

They were clearing up from breakfast. Norman heard water taps running, and the deep murmur of adult voices, some high, some low.

He walked up to the front door as if to leave the house but suddenly stepped into Barry's small office, which was to his right. He quickly opened up a drawer and removed the petty cash tin. He placed the tin carefully into the plastic bag which he put inside his satchel. As expected, it was a perfect fit.

He then walked out of the office, opened the front door and slipped out into the dark morning air, closing the door softly behind him.

He walked down the drive and for the first time in ages felt a great purpose about him. It was a rare feeling for Norman, rare indeed for many living in care. Norman half expected an enormous shout from behind to drag him back to the Home – but no such shout came.

The adventure was on.

He turned right at the end of the drive and then made two more rights.

At the mini-roundabout, there at the bottom of the Goldsworth Road, he failed to turn left to school as usual. Instead, he carried on forwards to Woking train station.

Just before he reached the station he darted behind a public toilet. He knelt down, removed the petty cash tin, and then he opened it.

He gulped. He had never seen quite so much money gathered in one place before. He stared at the pile for a bit. And then he picked out some coins and carefully put them into his trouser pocket.

He closed the tin, put it back in the plastic bag and satchel, and then emerged into the stream of the morning High Street.

He knew he was on the verge of something big yet it was funny to him how calm he was, as if God had placed him on automatic pilot.

He reached the ticket office, managed to get the word Guildford out to the bemused ticket man, handed over the coins in his pocket, took his ticket, walked onto the correct platform and waited for the silver machine.

When the train arrived, huffing and puffing and all out of breath, he hopped on. In a few hours he would be in Paris.

He was not quite yet a teenager.

* * *

On the train to Guildford he sat alone. Good. No one in sight. He opened up his satchel and pulled out the tin and the plastic bag. He opened the tin, took the money out, and put it all into the plastic bag.

The plastic bag then went back in the satchel. The empty petty cash tin he placed on the rack above him and hastily shoved out of sight.

He sat down and waited for Guildford to pull itself into view. Twenty minutes later, Guildford obliged. After leaving the train, he made his way to the nearby High Street, to Alders, the big department store.

Downstairs, a small passport office. It was nine thirty in the morning and Norman Bass's big moment had arrived.

He walked up to the window and asked for a 'one-one-one-one d-d-d-daa-yy-dayy passport.'

The cost was seventeen and six. Norman's money was all coins. It took him minutes to count out the right amount. Three pence, four pence, sixpence, a shilling…

You would have thought that the man taking the money might think to himself, here is a kid in his school uniform with an inordinate amount of money buying a one day passport, I should ring somebody. But the man cared not.

He was far more interested in the money than the child.

Having secured his pass, Norman walked back to Guildford station and caught the train to Dover. The journey took a couple of hours or so. He spent the time looking out of the window, watching the world flash by in streaks of green.

The voice above him came on. It said, we are now at Dover, our final destination. Norman gathered his things. He left the train and went to the harbour. He bought a ticket and still no one bothered him. He boarded the boat.

On the journey to France he suddenly realised that nearly all his money had gone. He shrugged his shoulders. What could he do?

The boat arrived in Calais. Norman joined the queue for customs. A man checked his passport and by the way he looked at him, for twenty excruciating seconds Norman truly believed the game was up.

But no, the passport was stamped and Norman was in France. Inside, his nerves were haywire. He was sure that at some point he would feel a hand on his shoulder and the adventure would be stopped.

But no such hand appeared.

He reached the end of the road, turned right and felt his nerves fly away into the blue tinged sky.

In front of him, the road into Calais. He marched into town, looked around. Nothing much to see. He got bored. So he moved on out of town and into the surrounding countryside. He saw an orchard and realised he was hungry.

He sneaked in, stole apples, and munched on them ravenously.

In a fashion, it sounded kind of idyllic, this little kid in the European sunshine, innocently walking through lush countryside, eating apples.

But life was rarely so kind. Or so pure.

Dusk approached, so he started hitching. Lorry drivers stopped to pick him up. But there was a price for their generosity. Sex was required. So Norman sat in the front seat, staring into darkness, white lines disappeared underneath him as his right hand caressed the driver's member.

Eventually, Norman reached Paris.

He did not do much sightseeing. A fellow traveller had told him about a road heading south out of the French capital where many hitchhikers gathered. That was where he had to get to.

When he found the meeting point, he found companionship. People said hello and did so warmly. They shared food and drink. He liked it here.

Words were not needed. People recognised their mutual needs. Norman felt a tinge of happiness, was glad to be where he was, began to think, they will have started the search for him in England by now – the fools: They would never think to search for him in France.

Norman got himself a lift. The man was going to the south of France. Again, with the lorry drivers, again with the hand jobs.

Soon, he was at the Spanish border. Norman thought, No turning back now, only forward.

But he had no passport, no papers, and very little money. Good. That made it all the more interesting. He surveyed the border points and realised that if he climbed a hill to the left of the border control without being noticed, he would be able to drop down into Spain.

He walked out of view of the patrolling officers, turned off the road, clambered up the hill and ran down. He heard a noise, looked right and saw a lorry approaching. He stuck his thumb out. The lorry stopped.

They drove for a bit and then Norman said, 'Where are we?'

And the driver replied, 'Spain.'

Blimey, Norman thought to himself that was quick. And easy. The driver now nudged Norman, gestured down to the middle of his open trousers. Norman did not flinch.

He travelled with the man for a bit, and then picked up another lorry.

Norman had by now decided to head for Alicante, halfway down the coastline he was travelling upon. He told the new driver his plan.

'Yes, yes,' the driver said smiling, 'but first let us stop at my house.'

Norman looked at him.

'To eat and drink,' the driver said laughing. Norman was reassured. He shouldn't have been.

They drove into a small village called Motril and pulled up outside a small cottage. Norman saw a wooden door. The driver got out and unlocked the door. Norman got out of the lorry and jumped down onto the gravel road. Stones splintered everywhere.

Norman entered the man's living quarters.

The apartment was small but presentable. 'Sit here,' the man said, and he pointed to a small sofa. He left the room and then a minute later came back in.

'Maybe you want the shower?' the man asked, and then added, 'after all your travelling.'

'Thank you,' said Norman. He felt tired and dirty. The chance to make himself clean was too good to miss.

'It is in there,' the man said and pointed to a door. 'I go and make the food.'

The man left the room. Norman stood, went through into the small bathroom.

He took off his clothes, carefully. He turned on the water and felt it with his hand until it was just right. He stepped in. The water poured onto his body and it made him feel great. He relaxed into the water, luxuriating in it. This was an unexpected luxury.

He lifted his head back and let the water drive into his face and then suddenly the man was standing beside him in the shower, naked with a look on his face that Norman really did not like.

At first, Norman was confused. He quickly stepped out of the shower and went into the bedroom. The man followed and pounced. He pushed Norman onto the bed so he was lying face down – and then he raped him.

The attack lasted just under three minutes, the worst three minutes in Norman Bass's life.

The man put on his clothes and then ordered Norman to get dressed. Norman did so in a silence that hung heavy with impurity, a silence moulded in fear.

Then the man went to the front door and opened it. He gestured for Norman to leave. Norman walked through the door back onto the gravel road which seemed to shriek in pain under his step. The door slammed.

Norman walked slowly down the dusty street, so frightened, so scared. He could not look at the men who passed him by on the street. He lowered his head as they passed, creating his own symbol of shame. What if it happened again, he thought to himself? Or what if worse occurred?

Who could he turn to? Who could he run to?

Norman now fully comprehended the consequence of his actions. And they were vast and startling. He saw himself as he really was, a small boy alone in a huge world without any protection from the lustful, the murderous, the wolves, who would consume him in a second.

He had never felt so terrified in his whole life.

On all levels – physically, mentally and spiritually – he was so close to shutting down.

He reached the small town square and, to his joy, he saw a policeman standing on the other side of the square. Please notice me, Norman thought to himself. Please, please notice me.

He continually sent this thought in the direction of the policeman, prayed that his distress signal would alert him.

The action worked. The policeman walked over to Norman and spoke to him. In Spanish.

'English,' Norman said repeatedly, 'English.'

'Pasaporte,' the policeman repeatedly said, 'pasaporte.'

Norman shook his head. 'I don't have one,' he told the policeman.

The policeman looked at him in amazement.

Half an hour later, Norman Bass was in the local police cell.

Norman lived in this cell for a week whilst the authorities tried to figure out how a little boy from England had crossed two borders without a passport. Incredible.

The cleaner in the police station took pity on him. Coffee and doughnuts magically appeared at Norman's cell window every morning.

Then dysentery struck him, placed him in absolute agony. Every cloud has a silver lining. His virulent illness hurried his return to England. Two days after contracting this illness, Norman was bound for Burbank.

On arrival in the UK, he was taken to a hospital where it took him a week to recover from his illness.

The recovered Norman was then brought back to Burbank, back to where he once belonged.

Of course, he was expecting the worse; a barrage of shouting and anger from Barry, it went without saying.

But his illness seemed to have dulled their angry annoyance with him. In fact, everyone was quite nice to him. He liked the feeling, liked the attention.

He suddenly started thinking, you know what, let me just belong. Let me become part of the whole. Somebody, please be my friend, and let life be normal. But then he opened his mouth and he stammered, and he could not let people know how he felt, and he knew then that he would always be the outsider.

Barry made an unusual move. He asked Norman to write down all his experiences during his time on the run onto sheets of white paper. Put it down in ink, Barry said to him, because it will be good for you.

Norman started writing. He recalled little about the trip except his route: Calais, Paris, Marseille, down the coast over the mountains, Spain, oh and the fact that he had been raped.

He took the paper to Barry, handed it over and walked away. He thought nothing more of the exercise until suddenly Barry appeared and waved the paper violently in the air, screamed and shouted, with specks of angry spit flecking his beard as he demanded to know what the hell had happened in Spain.

Norman said nothing.

A day later, Norman was taken to a sexual disease clinic in nearby Guildford and thoroughly examined. He was passed clean. Norman travelled back to Burbank and a week later did what he did best. He ran away again. Couldn't stand all the shouting, he said to me.

Only this time, he ran to one specific place, his home, to his parents, to where he began in life.

To the authorities that was deemed a very significant action. The boy was saying he wanted to go home.

The authorities told Norman he could go home at weekends and school holidays. They believed that contact with his family would heal the scars and maybe his runaway nature.

They never thought once to look at his stammer.

His parents had acquired a new house and Norman was given his own bedroom. Still, it was not enough. He could not help himself. The urge to run persisted. He could not help himself. Every week, he ran away from home. Every week, his parents came and collected him. Just like the old days.

On one occasion, he ended up in Brighton. He sat in the police station and waited for his parents to come. Only this time a policeman told Norman he was not going home. He was being sent back to Burbank. His parents could take no more.

As he digested the news, Barry arrived.

On the drive home, Norman remembered that he looked over at Barry and noted that Barry actually seemed upset that things had not worked out for Norman. Then he closed his eyes.

When he woke up, it was back to life at Burbank again.

* * *

Norman revealed his story to me with a stoic equanimity. The rape, the abuse, the horror of it all, at no point did he break. At no point did the voice quiver or the eyes water.

Instead, he told me how all his life he asked himself one question – why did no one address the problem of his stammer? Why had no one talked to him about it?

It was so obvious that this was the cause of all his ills yet no staff member, teacher, authority figure ever broached the subject.

That was until he met a child psychologist named Dr Barnes.

Dr Barnes worked at a child guidance clinic that Norman attended after school.

Unlike others, Dr Barnes showed understanding, great sympathy.

'I used to like collecting lizards when I lived in Camberley,' Norman said. 'I got quite good at it. I used to breed them as well. I expressed this interest to her and one day I went over there and instead of sitting doing tests in a classroom, she came out with a packed lunch and said, today we are going to go and collect lizards.

'We spent the afternoon together. I showed her how you catch them and what you do and we had a fantastic day.'

Norman's confidence picked up a bit. Quite a bit, in fact. He even got himself a girlfriend.

'I can't remember her name now,' he said smiling, 'but for some reason she liked me and we started going out. I thought I should tell somebody at Burbank that I was seeing somebody because they always wanted to know where you are going. I finally got up the courage to speak to Julie and told her I had a girl. Suddenly, it was action stations.

'At Burbank, a lot of us had to wear hand me down clothes but Barry took me to a menswear shop near the station and I have never had so much clothing bought for me in all my life. He got me a blue Budgie jacket, tank top jumpers, Oxford bag trousers. I looked the dog's bollocks. It was great. I remember I had to parade around the sitting room with my new clobber in front of all the older girls and they were all saying how good I looked.

'I went on the date, all very civilised. I think we might have held hands but you can imagine what I was like. Totally nervous, stammering away, no experience around girls. I didn't tell her I lived in a home.'

A couple of weeks later Julie suggested Norman invited his girlfriend to tea. Norman took to the idea and, on their next date together, he asked her. This took courage for it meant you had to tell someone you were in care.

She probably knew anyway, I told Norman. At school, you could not keep your home life a secret. Too many questions needed answering. Two in particular always floored me. 'Where do you live?' was one and, 'What do your mum and dad do?' was the other.

'At school I didn't tell anyone I was in a home apart from a couple of really close mates,' he revealed. 'It wasn't shame but a lot of them wouldn't have understood. You know what it's like with kids, anything out of the ordinary and they take the piss out of you all day long.

'Anyway she came up to Burbank and she was allowed to go through the front door, which was a great honour. We always had to go through the back door. I thought to myself, you don't know what has just happened here.

'I sat at Barry's table with her and he started taking the piss out of me. Not in a horrible way but constantly. Then he began teasing her as well. Have you kissed him yet? All that kind of thing. Then we went for a walk and from the top window of the house you can see the whole of the garden, I can remember to this day Maggie watching me from that window, putting me under constant surveillance.'

The girl ended the relationship soon after this visit. You could not blame her. The strangeness of it all had no doubt unnerved her. Norman's response was simple. He started running abroad again.

'One time I got as far as Monaco where the policeman just took me to the outskirts of the city and said, that way,' Norman said. 'I ended up in Marseille and gave myself up. Got no money, no passport.

'I remember I had to go for an interview and it was the same guy who had come to Spain. He recognised me and he told me that a new rule had now been put in place by the local county council. Part of my punishment was that I now had to repay the fare to get me home.'

And then Norman turned sixteen and left school. He was now obliged to leave Burbank.

At that time, the council were no longer legally obliged to house or feed any child after they left education. That person was now of work age and therefore responsible for himself.

The good old days.

'I was sad to leave Burbank,' Norman said. 'I had been there for five years. In fact, I felt really desolate because I no longer had a safety net. I realised then that Barry, the social workers, all of them, had missed the point.

'None of them had worked out why I was doing what I was doing and now I was going straight back to the environment where it all started with nothing resolved and no help given.

'Burbank was good from a practical level. There was a roof over my head, regular meals, I got clothed, there was schooling but there was no intimate "Let's see if we can work through this together." Apart from that one woman who was the only one who spent some time with me.'

The only choice Norman had was to head home to his parents, the original source of his unhappiness. Once there, of course, he started running away again. One time, he lived in a friend's house under the very nose of the unsuspecting mother.

'I used to sleep under his bed,' Norman said. 'The mum was out at work all day so I would get up after she had gone and then just hang out.

'Then I got busted for stealing milk off a doorstep. That was my first criminal offence. Anyway this guy came and picked me up from the station and instead of taking me home he took me to a hostel in Woking called Verrells.'

Verrells was run by a man named Mr Gallagher. His job was to provide for kids still subject to a care order but in employment. Gallagher was tough, not afraid to take you into his office and give you a slap, as Norman discovered.

Norman found work at a fencing manufacturer in nearby, Brookwood. He would come home stinking of creosote. All the kids complained so he was given his own room. That was about the only good thing that happened to him at Verrells.

Then he turned eighteen and that was it, he was no longer the local council's responsibility or a ward of care. Norman Bass was out on his own.

* * *

Lunch arrived. The sandwiches were eaten, the talk between us was genial. The tension created by his rape story had dissipated, gone. Again, care had bonded us. I recalled Norman talked proudly about his life now, showed me photos of dear loved ones.

He asked about my life but I gave short answers. I wanted to keep him focussed on his own adventures. But then something occurred to me.

'Norman,' I said, 'If you stole the petty cash tin, then it stands to reason that it must have been you who purloined my Churchill coin. You are the thief. You are the man who took away my fortune.'

'Sorry about that,' he said with a little smile.

'As it is you, I'll let you off the thirty thousand pounds you owe me,' I replied. 'Let's carry on with the interview.'

After Verrells, chaos. Norman got married three times, bore a daughter named Nicky, who he sees regularly.

With his ex-wives, there is no such contact. There was, however, drunkenness, infidelity, the normal broken tapestry relationships that most of us in care look for when we enter the world.

How could it not be so?

Most of us leave care with our wiring made haywire. It takes years to repair the damage. In many cases, recovery is not even made.

An addiction to chaos was a major problem. We couldn't shake it off or make ourselves resistant to its demands. We had been raised in chaos and so without it we were lost. We yearned for chaos. After all, it had been the only constant in our journey.

'I started going from one relationship to another,' Norman said. 'I craved one to one intimacy but in relationships I would use people up. It would get to a point where I would think, this has run out, what do I do next?'

I knew fear of intimacy would be a common factor between the two of us. It always is for us motherless children. Norman's played out in exactly the same fashion as mine did. You chase the girl, you get the girl, you dump the girl. Why?

Because it was the *chasing* rather than the getting, that provided the biggest thrill.

In this arena, deep hatred of self ran the show.

Example: Someone said, I love you. Your inner pattern read, Well, I am worthless. So you must be lower than I am to love someone as worthless as me. And because of that I am going to reject you.

We were emotional vampires. We sucked what we wanted out of people, got bored, then moved on. But if we were lucky, and if we went searching, we would be given a moment that changed our lives.

'One day, I realised that I wanted to do a job where people were in a situation worse than I am,' he said. 'It was simple as that but it changed so much.'

In that moment of clarity and realisation, Norman determined he would dedicate himself to the helping of others. He would now become the saint not the sinner.

'So I got a job in a home in Bracknell, Surrey, for adults with learning disabilities. I worked there for a year but it was very institutionalised. Because I wasn't qualified on paper to do this kind of work I now went from one care job to another. I actually worked in a children's home in Cheshire.'

Norman loved the Home. It was brand new, designed as the first stop for kids coming into care.

It didn't escape Norman's attention how things had changed for the better within the care system. More staff, fewer kids was one significant development. And there was a completely different environment from the often chaotic one at Burbank.

Norman then got lucky. Really lucky. He met Tania. They met when Norman was out canvassing for the church he attended. He rang on Tania's doorbell and not long after saw her at mass. They got talking, and as they did, love got to work.

'She and my other partners were as different as chalk and cheese,' Norman said brightly. 'When Tania and my daughter Nicky met it was like they had known each other for years. Tania is very motherly. She has got a child of her own and they clicked.

'They were going into Mothercare together, the whole bit. I thought this is exactly what Nicky needs, someone to be alongside her. That made me very happy. I think now that there was definitely an element about being in care that impacted on my marriages.

'I was not a rooted person, I did not have family values and I was transient. Now I can say that all the ingredients I have been craving for so long are all together.'

'What are those ingredients?' I asked. Late afternoon shadows were now dropping onto our faces.

Norman considered my question.

Then he said, 'I know now that I have the love and respect of my partner Tania, and her little boy, and I have got grandchildren now. My daughter is fantastic, my work life is amazing. I am a principal carer in a company. We are given care via the primary health trust of children that have long-term health issues. I feel wanted now and I feel appreciated.

'I have come out of that children's home environment and I have achieved so much. I was thinking the other day that for a long time I really didn't know what I was looking for. But now being that much older I know I can't go for something new all the time. When I got together with Tania I told her I really don't care what job I do, just as long as I am with you. It sounds soppy but as it turns out I got my cake and I am eating it because I have a fantastic home life and a fantastic job. And I don't stammer anymore.'

I was coming onto that.

'Know what happened?'

'Tell all,' I said.

'I went to a church in Aldershot and I was invited to go to the front and receive healing for my stammer. Whether I received it or not I couldn't say but it was round about that time that I began to realise that I could speak for more than one sentence without breaking out into a cold sweat. It was pretty instantaneous.

'One day I am a gibbering wreck who can't speak to anyone through the glass at a post office and the next I can ring up people and talk to them about all kinds of things and am able to walk into a room and talk to seven hundred people.'

Norman looked at the clock. 'Tania will be home soon,' he said and suddenly, he looked a bit worried.

I asked why.

'Tania had a wonderful childhood,' he explained. 'Her parents were fantastic people, there were no upsets, she was really loved, so when I talk about my past she sometimes…'

'Breaks into tears?' I asked. 'Don't worry, it will be fine,' I assured him. 'We are basically finished although one more question. Was living at Burbank, living in care, good or bad for you?'

'Overall, I consider myself very fortunate,' he replied. 'I am *where* I am and *who* I am despite being in care, but also because of it. Does that make sense?' he asked.

'Generally, yes,' I replied.

'You know, even though my somewhat innocent and naïve recollections about Burbank have been blown away, I still think it was a relatively good thing for me personally. If I think about the possibility of what may have happened to me *without* being in care, well, it makes me shudder.'

I switched off the tape. I stood, gathered my things and extended my hand. Norman warmly shook it. A taxi was called. It arrived within the minute.

'See you later, bruv,' Norman Bass said to me by his front door.

'I'll be back before you know it,' I told him.

'I'd like that very much,' he said.

Norman Bass has many things now. He has love and trust and respect but more importantly, he has knowledge of self.

So much of the orphan life is spent in confusion. Why is this happening to me? Why did I get it in the neck? Why am I being treated like this and no one else?

Why do I make actions which only serve to hurt me?

Those questions were gone now. They no longer haunted him. Norman Bass, after years of misery, had happiness – and he wore it well.

It made me so pleased for him.

Like I said, remarkable.

* * *

Norman noted Paolo staring deeply into his eyes. He had just told him about the rape in Spain and he knew exactly what Paolo was thinking. He was trying to figure out if the incident still haunted him, whether it was still of great emotional disturbance within his soul.

You can look all you like, Norman thought, but you won't see anything and that is because I have dealt with it. The memory is burnt out, no longer able to attack me with ferocity.

Norman had enjoyed the day, enjoyed going over his life. He liked Paolo, he liked how he allowed him to speak without interruption.

He even liked the pretentious little Oscar Wilde type quotes he kept throwing at him.

Only one thing perturbed Norman. It was that moment in their talk when Paolo realised that Norman had inadvertently stolen his Churchill Crown.

Although the man had made light of the incident, Norman had detected a hurt in Paolo's eyes. Not a big hurt but a hurt all the same.

And so an idea struck.

After Paolo left, Norman turned on the internet and tapped the phrase Churchill Crown into Google.

Numerous websites came up in front of him. He read about the coin's history and its current value. Today, the Churchill Crown's value is precisely twenty-five pence. Not £30,000. He smiled and bought himself one.

The next day he bought a card. On it he wrote, 'Sorry I kept this for so long.'

When the coin arrived, he put coin and card in the post, special delivery.

Two days later, there was a red note on Paolo's doormat, telling him to go and pick up a parcel.

He figured it must be the books he had recently ordered.

He walked to the post office. He stood in a line. He was given his package.

Then he did something out of the usual for him. He opened up the package, there and then. No idea why. Normally, he waited until he got home. But something in his mind told him to look now.

He tore apart the paper. For a second he had no idea what he was holding. Then he read Norman's card.

As much as he wanted to hold the tears back, Paolo could not do so. A slight river slid down his cheek, and that river, slow and careful, would not stop until he had reached the safety of his home.

Norman's act of kindness, the depth and meaning behind his action, was of immeasurable value.

Paolo sat on his sofa, and he looked at that coin for ages before he picked up his mobile and texted Norman. He wrote: 'Norman, what I hold in my hand now is one of the best presents I have ever been given.'

And he truly meant that.

For Father Tucker was right.

The coin had proved to be worth an absolute fortune.

From: paolo@gmail.com

To: desh@hotmail.com

Subject: RE: The New Book

Des – Hope all well, amico. Just to say that in doing research for the book, two men have become heroes to me – they are Thomas Coram who created Britain's first ever children's home, http://en.wikipedia.org/wiki/Thomas_Coram – and John Barnardo – http://www.infed.org/thinkers/barnardo.htm – who of course created the Barnardo's Homes. Both of these men were pioneers and blessed with great courage and compassion. Their achievements are really worth exploring if you get the time. They were men who left the world in a much better shape and without them the likes of us would have been so much poorer. I know what you mean about putting the reader off with history lessons but I think this is a valuable and fascinating history and as one of the aims of this book is to open up the children's home to the wider world, perhaps it needs saying. I have just been to see Norman Bass. I am sure you remember him – had a stutter and always ran away. I had a great day with him. He had been through so much but seemed very much at peace with life. I was so anxious that at the start of this all the stories would be doom and gloom but half way through and everything remains very positive. Makes me happy and, yes, very proud. David Westbrook is next. He e-mailed me yesterday. (Would this book have existed without the internet, I wonder?) Up the Spurs. Paolo

Three

The Boy Who Couldn't Be Heard

The Story of David Westbrook

Unhappy children steal. I certainly did.

First thing in the morning, when my foster mother was busy getting dressed, I would sneak downstairs, and take money from her brown leather purse. A halfpenny at first, then a penny, a sixpence, and then onwards, to my greatest prize, a half crown coin.

I couldn't help myself.

Inevitably, I was caught. I think that was the first time she stripped me of my clothing, laid me over the dinner table, and caned me.

No lesson was learnt. My life still revolved around stealing. On the way to school I snatched newspapers from the mouths of front doors and milk from their feet.

I dived into the local sweet shop and snaffled bars of chocolate. At school, I waited for class to begin and then pretended I needed the toilet. Toilet, schmoilet.

Soon as I was out of the classroom door, I was in the cloakroom rifling through my fellow pupils' jacket pockets. In PE lessons, I was always the last one to get undressed. Why? Because it gave me a minute or so in an empty changing room full of tempting grey trousers and blue blazers.

When I arrived at Burbank Children's Home, in the April of 1968, I was ten years old and a thief of admirable consistency.

But then my burgeoning career as a thief came to an abrupt end. One night, my pal Lazlo Molnar and I robbed Woking Football Club. As the players trained on the pitch, we rifled through their clothes.

We got a wallet containing fifty pounds. We were both twelve years old. Two weeks later the police arrested us. I faced the worst punishment I could imagine: expulsion from my school, St John the Baptist Secondary in Woking.

I could not face life without my school friends. They were my family. I'd already lost one set. No way could I afford to lose another. So I stopped stealing. Except for the odd moment in my twenties and early thirties, when I would unexpectedly find myself walking out of a shop with an unpaid newspaper or a magazine under my jumper, sharp nerves soaring through me.

'Why did you do that?' my partner asked when I showed her my bounty.

'Do you know, I have no idea,' I said, secretly exhilarated.

David Westbrook also stole. He stole like I did. Except there was a difference: his stealing got him into prison.

* * *

We met at Guildford train station. The day was bright and hot. The trees and flowers were in blossom. David was waiting in his car by the station entrance. When I saw him he had the most lovely smile on his face.

I climbed inside and we shook hands, firmly.

He set off. Talk was easy. One of the first questions he asked was, 'How do you remember me?'

'As a really naughty boy,' I said. 'If I recall correctly, you always seemed to be getting caught for stealing.'

'That's right, but a lot of the time I didn't do it. See, I just wanted…'

'Not now,' I said, 'Just keep driving and save it for the interview.'

He had obviously been rehearsing his lines for our talk.

David was a long-term resident at Burbank. During my time there I shared a bedroom with David and six other kids. Later on, the two of us shared a smaller bedroom.

David was three years younger than me, so at first I didn't have that much to do with him. Perhaps this was why when I recalled him, my mind's eye had gone hazy.

David's recollections of me were far more vivid.

Driving to his house where he lived with his wife Margaret and adopted daughter, Dionne, he told me that I had taught him how to box.

This was shocking news to me. I am neither violent nor a skilled fighter. Yet David insisted I had taught him to jab with his left and then punch with his right. He told me that one day at school he had tried out this combination and floored some poor unfortunate kid with one punch.

He told me that in the bedroom we shared together, I continually played him Faces and David Bowie records – now that sounded right – and that the first time he ever got drunk was with me and my schoolmate Sean O'Flaherty.

The pair of us had apparently taken David to a nearby pub and got him goggle-eyed and crazy on beer. (Light and bitter, most probably.) He remembered after the second pint, Sean and I demanding that he buy a round, and that the price came to seventy-six pence.

David would find no problem getting his round in now. He runs a successful air conditioning business and in a good year clears a six figure salary.

More importantly, David had found love. Margaret. He phoned her twice during the twenty minute journey to his house. Just to make sure she was okay.

At first, I was a little scornful of his devotion but throughout the day I became fascinated by it. Love seemed to have lightened his load. It had been the same with Norman Bass.

A lesson was being delivered.

We pulled up at his four-bedroom house on the outskirts of Guildford. A concrete mixer stood in front of his house and some workman's tools lay haphazardly on his driveway.

'The builders are in,' he said. He got out of the car. So did I. He spoke across the roof of the car. 'I'm having loads done to the house.'

Margaret opened the door. David smiled.

'This is Paolo,' he said, I think a little proudly. 'Known him a million years.'

'Lovely to meet you,' she said. 'Come in.'

Margaret had seen me on the TV the night before and was highly complimentary, insisting how well I had done in life. I smiled inwardly at the irony. At that point in my life, I was financially hurting and all ends up in a major relationship. I was living day to day, just hoping to get through the mess my chaos had created.

Yet I totally understood Margaret's view. If I saw anyone on television, my first thought is that their life must be wonderful, joyous, secure forever. They were on the box, they were on TV. Therefore, they must be more than all right. I accepted Margaret's compliments and said nothing.

We went through to the kitchen where tea was brewed, chit chat was exchanged.

Eventually, Margaret said, 'I'll leave you to it,' and exited stage right, leaving just David, myself and a tape recorder. The large kitchen was dominated by a wooden table. I sat at one end, David the other.

He was dressed in non-descript clothes. Shapeless shirt, blue jeans. His hair was mousy; his build was like mine except his stomach was slightly protruding. He wore glasses and still carried the freckles on his cheeks that I recalled from our time at Burbank.

Behind me, I heard the builders in the garden doing that which David had paid them to do.

I pressed the record button. 'Nervous?' I asked.

'Not a bit.'

'Good. So let's start at the beginning. How did you come to be in care?'

He came to be in care because his mum and dad were teenagers when they conceived him. Mother was fourteen, father was fifteen.

It was 1960. Shame and scandal. No way would they be given charge of their child.

'I haven't got a clue who my mum and dad were,' he said. 'I don't even know their names; I am still in the dark because I couldn't get my social services report. I tried to get it recently but they say it's been lost so there you go.

'I spent my first year at a place called Abeath, which was a nursery place in Woking, Surrey,' David said. 'From there I was adopted. My new parents were Westbrooks and we lived at number thirty, York Road, Woking.'

'So Westbrook isn't really your surname?' I asked.

'That's right,' he replied.

First connection – Hewitt isn't my proper surname either, I told him. The name belonged to my mother's first husband, not my blood father.

'Unfortunately,' David said, 'I was ill-treated by my adopted mother and that's why I was taken into care. She used to beat me so I was carted off to a place called Woodrough in Bramley, near Guildford when I was about three years old.

'Woodrough was a holding place. I don't remember much about it except these huge black windows with a catch on them and that *Batman* was on the TV and we used to get raincoats and run around the garden pretending we were Batman. I don't know how long I was there for but from there I ended up at Burbank, which was a permanent place.'

Again, huge similarities. I too had been beaten by a foster parent. I too had been thrown out of the family home and into care. Like Norman Bass I had been placed at Woodrough whilst the county council decided my fate.

David was different to Norman and me, though.

He didn't cry his eyes out when he was forced to move to Burbank.

Woodrough had not impacted on him in the same way it did Norman and me. He did not open himself up to anybody at Woodrough. The barriers he had erected inside of himself, built from massive distrust and fear, were just too formidable to crack open in such a short time.

At Burbank, though, a different story.

At Burbank, he eased up, started to enjoy himself.

Unlike Woodrough, there were numerous kids his own age to befriend and run around with.

'We had loads of adventures,' he enthusiastically said. 'Do you remember those bamboos at the bottom of the garden?

We demolished them. We were in the garden one day and Stephen B. said, "Look, what I've just found." It was a box of matches. So we gathered up some leaves in the bamboos and we lit a fire.

'Next thing we know the bamboos have gone bang and Maggie (staff member) came rushing down and then called the fire brigade. That night Barry came home and I was cacking myself. Do you remember how he used to come right up to your face and scream at you?'

Did I ever. At first Barry's shouting badly frightened me. Then my friend Colin N. told me to take a step back and look at how funny his contorted face became, like a clown on LSD.

From then on the fear was gone. In fact, it was all I could do to not burst out laughing every time Barry leant forward and bellowed at me. I have loved Colin all my life for giving me that valuable life-lesson.

'He screamed at me and told me to get to bed,' David said. 'But the good thing about it is that the next day it was forgotten. It wasn't something they played on, which was great.

'We used to mess around in the garden all the time,' David said. 'Then smoking came into the equation. I think I was about nine or ten. There were more packets of fags in that garden than there were in the shop down the road.

'I remember Barry one day seeing them all and making me Fred and Stephen go round the garden and pick them all up. Then he said I want you to bring the rubbish up to the house. We put it outside the house. Then he got all the older boys, I think you were included as well, and he said, right you lot are going to eat all these packets of fags...'

I'll give him one thing – Barry was certainly consistent in his punishments. He did exactly the same thing to me after seeing me in a phone box with a packet of Number Six cigarettes clearly visible in my top jacket pocket.

David started his primary school education at St Dunstan's School in Woking. It was a thirty minute walk away from Burbank. I too went to St Dunstan's. I loved my time there.

David didn't fare so well. He hit a fellow pupil over the head with a table tennis bat and was quickly shunted off to Barnsbury School down the road. Soon after his arrival they caught him smoking. He was nine years old.

'The headmaster Mr Burbage called me into his office,' David recalls, 'and he said, "Right Westbrook, you want to smoke, smoke these." And he gave me a cigar. Thing is I really enjoyed it! But I got ill-treated all the time at that school. I felt Mr Burbage would find any excuse to give me the slipper. I think because I was in a home. I felt victimised all the time.'

This is a regular theme for care kids. All of us, at some point, had to deal with the brutish assumptions of others, had to face down those who truly believed that we were deserving of our fate, who truly thought our broken childhoods were our fault. To this day I still come across them. And my heart goes out to them.

Imagine having to go through life carrying such a mean spirit.

'I wasn't a goody-goody but I wasn't a baddy-baddy either,' David said, 'although Maggie who was a staff member certainly thought so.'

I remembered Maggie, well. She was a thin Scottish woman, extremely pale skinned, red haired, with glasses. She reminded me a lot of my foster mum, always seemed so unhappy, so on edge, always looked for any chance she could get to shout and bawl one of us out.

David felt her wrath, her bitter anger.

'Do you remember those bins out by the kitchen?' David asked me. 'I had to clean them up every morning. That was my job. Then you had to get a member of staff to check it and once they said it was okay, you could get your breakfast.'

'As you know, breakfast was served at a certain time and if you didn't get there by a certain time, you would miss out on the cereals and I love cereal.

'One day I had done my job and done it really well. The place was spotless. You could have eaten your dinner off those rubbish bins. I got into the queue for breakfast cereal and I was just about to get my bowl when Maggie said, "Have you done your job?" I said yes, she said, "Let's go and check."

'We go round there and all the bins had been turned upside down. There was rubbish everywhere. She went absolutely mental. I don't know how it happened, but to this day I reckon it was her. That's how evil she was. I was out there for half an hour picking all the rubbish up again.'

The day Maggie left the Home was a relief to all, including, I wouldn't mind betting, some of the other staff members, such was her tetchy and aggressive demeanour.

I remembered too the jobs we were given every week – peeling potatoes, washing up, doing the boiler, sweeping up outside. Yet, compared to the long hours that my foster mother made me labour, those jobs were easy, over and done within half an hour at the most.

But if the purpose of this work was to install discipline, then in David's case it failed. Magnificently. He started to rebel, started to steal, as all unhappy children tend to do.

Then he made another discovery and it would prove fatal.

'Do you remember how if anything went wrong, Barry and Sandy would call everyone into the dining room and you weren't allowed to move until someone owned up?' David asked me.

Of course, I replied. I can still remember the tension filling up that room as all of us waited to see who would admit to the crime in question and be publicly punished.

I remembered your hand being raised a lot on such occasions, I told David.

He chuckled at my memory but then frowned.

'Okay, sometimes it was me,' he confessed, 'but I didn't do half of the things I owned up to.'

I was confused. Then why confess?

'To get attention,' David said. 'I wanted attention. No one was giving me any attention so I owned up to things I did not do. And because of that I started being accused of stuff. It was just seeking the attention.'

I had been lucky. At Burbank I was seen as a bright kid, one with a future. Attention came to me. David was not so fortunate. A lot of the time he was passed over. Twenty-five children lived at Burbank. Someone would have to go to the back of the queue.

David's yearning for attention was to have terrible consequences for him. As he kept owning up to things he did not do, the perception of him as a child beyond help persuaded his carers that he needed a different environment to help change his ways.

David was taken out of school and moved to Barnum's, a Borstal school for maladjusted kids. Barnum's was an absolute roughhouse. Violence provided the institution's crooked energy.

It occurred on a massive scale.

I wasn't surprised to hear David now talk about staff members assaulting him.

Borstal schools were fearsome institutions. Violence came at you from all sides. Could be from the staff, could be from each other. Did not matter.

'I used to have a problem wetting the bed as a kid,' David said. 'At Burbank it was easy, it got dealt with. If I wet the bed at Barnum's I was stood at the end of the bed naked and a staff member would come in and punch me in the stomach for no reason.

'I remember going back to Burbank once with a severely protruding lip where a staff member at the school had hit me and no one did anything about it. No one listened. In the end, I thought okay, I'll get in trouble with the police and then perhaps that way someone will listen. So I got in trouble with the police.'

During one vacation, David and a fellow Burbankian, Peter, burgled a local house, stole fifty pounds. That was quite a sum back then. They managed a trip to the pictures before they were apprehended by the police. Silly boys, they had left their fingerprints everywhere.

Yet they were not silly. David had succeeded because again he had garnered some kind of attention. Sure, he was in trouble but at least someone was talking to him.

Unfortunately for David, Burbank was not impressed with this turn of events. In the staff's eyes, he was simply too much of a handful and they washed their hands off him. No more holidays at Burbank.

'Burbank booted me out and I ended up in a place called Kinton,' David said.

At Kinton, David Westbrook learnt more about crime in a year than you and I will do in a lifetime. He had just taken his first step towards prison.

* * *

If life at Burbank was occasionally harsh, the regime at Kinton was unremitting in its cruelty. The school once made the national newspapers when the head forced a pupil to bend over and then allowed all staff and inmates to hit him with a slipper.

The boy received sixty blows.

'You had these masters who basically kicked the shit out of you,' David explained. 'If you did something wrong, they attacked you. We are not talking a couple of slaps here and there, it would be fists and feet.'

One time, David said, he was smoking in the dining room with some other boys, when a staff member came up from behind and kneed him so badly in the back, he crumpled to the floor.

When the pain subsided, David stood up, picked up a chair and attempted to smash it over the man's head.

Surrounded and hemmed in by such violence, it was not surprising that David started running away. When he was caught, he gave social services a graphic account of the abuse and violence at Kinton.

But, again, no one attended to his desperate words.

Of course, they did not. He was the boy no one listened to.

'The only good thing about Kinton,' he said, 'was that there was a Mr Marshall, and he was a decent bloke. He used to take me out and one day he bought a local paper and there was a company advertising in it for a refrigeration air conditioner trainee. He said, phone them up. Basically, they were building a Fine Fare superstore right in the middle of Woking and needed people. I went for the interview and got the job, twelve pounds a week.

'This guy I was working for then said to me, "Do you want to go to college and learn the trade? I'll give you a wage increase of twenty-two pounds." I said, done. That is the only thing I got from Kinton, a trade, the one thing that has seen me through to my life today. Now, I am doing a hundred thousand pounds job so that is the only thing I can say Kinton has done for me. The rest was a nightmare.'

The catch was that Kinton insisted David handed his wages to them every week. In return, he would be given back maybe a tenth of what he had earned. The rest of the money simply disappeared.

David calculated that if ten of the inmates were having their wage packets lightened in a similar manner, the staff at Kinton embezzled around about five hundred pounds a week, a huge sum in the early seventies.

David continued playing truant.

'I found pubs and clubs and I used to stay out, never go back,' he said.

'I would stay at friends' houses or stay with women I knew. One week at work I worked sixty-six hours and I got paid nearly seventy-two pounds. No way was I going to give Kinton that amount so I doctored the wage slip.

'I changed the amount from seventy-two to twenty-two and then gave it to the woman at Kinton. She didn't notice a thing. I thought great, so every week I started doing the same thing – doing overtime then changing the wage details on the brown packet they gave you. Kinton could not understand how I was pissed as a fart every night on about two pounds a week.'

Alcohol did for David. Most nights he took a holiday from himself and his world, sought relief in the warmth and the promise of a better time that the drink gave him every night without fail.

He started turning up late for his job. His work suffered. His boss got angry. The sack was quick in coming.

David had no money. He turned to crime.

'It was things like breaking into shops, stealing and then flogging the gear on,' he confesses. 'I remember we broke into this sex shop one night. Now I had never seen a dildo before and the bloke I was with told me it was a tea-stirrer. We got away, went to the pub and I went up to the bar lady, showed her the dildo and said do you want to buy a tea stirrer? The woman looked at it and said, give me two!'

Out of the blue a job offer in Liverpool came through, again refrigeration. David was seventeen-and-a-half. He ran away from Kinton and headed north to Liverpool, where he took the job. Six months later the police arrested him for a minor offence. But by then it was too late. David was eighteen and no longer a ward of the council. Kinton had no hold of him now. He'd escaped. He had a new town, and a new career as a criminal to consider.

* * *

Fuck you. As a child, you deny me love, you deny me attention, you deny me security. Therefore, you must think me the lowest of the low. Fine. I'll show you how low I can go. I'll go to places you haven't even dreamt about, I'll prove to you just how unhappy I am. I'll act in ways that will shock you to your safe little heart and then when you try to stop me, I'll tell you again. Fuck you.

No one had listened to the child, so the man took over and he said, fuck you a million times to all forms of authority.

David Westbrook became a full-time criminal, went into credit fraud with a friend of his.

'How did that work?' I asked him. I was intrigued. Crime does that to me.

'Easy, you open up accounts in thirty-two different banks under thirty-two different names. You put in a hundred pounds in the first account and keep moving the money around,' he explained.

'Keep that up for a couple of months and then you say to the bank I need a cheque guarantee card. They then send you one. So now you've got thirty-two cheque books and thirty-two cards. Every day we would go to a bank and draw out money. That was our job. Going to the bank every day, opening up accounts and drawing out money.'

'Nice work if you can get it,' I remarked.

'It is until you get caught,' he drily replied.

'I went into the bank one day and I was collared. At the police station, I had never seen so many cheques in all my life. But I only owned up to two. I just went that one is mine, that one is mine, the rest I don't know about. The police were so primitive in those days, they didn't have a clue. These days if you wrote something out, they would send it to an expert and have you. In those days, it was quick arrest, quick conviction. I got a three month suspended sentence. I never gave them the guy I was doing it with. I told them I didn't know his name.'

David and his partner in crime celebrated with champagne and women. Yet there was something else going on at this time, something very specific to orphans.

David trusted no one. As far as he was concerned, everyone – his partner, his lovers, his friends – was out to get him and, therefore, everyone was under suspicion.

I too have felt the same way. So have a million other orphans. You cannot blame us. One can only take so many knife wounds to the back.

'If I met someone and had known him for years, I still wouldn't trust the clothes on his back,' David said. 'That's the way I was. Even the guy I was doing cheques with, I didn't trust him one bit. I used to sit down with him and we would have a laugh saying, this time next year we will be millionaires. But I never trusted him, never trusted anyone.'

In other words, fuck you. Except now David had a much bigger problem than issues based around lack of trust and intimacy.

The police had his name and number and they were on his trail.

David had come to their attention because with some of the proceeds of his cheque scam, he had bought a motor bike. Fine. Except, one day he went flying off the bike at top speed, broke bones and cracked open skin.

When he woke up in hospital, he was told the police had been asking questions. He took in that information, recovered, and then hi-tailed it back to Woking to avoid having to explain himself to the authorities.

The Liverpool police charged him with reckless driving anyway. A court date was set. In Woking, David now realised he did not have the money to make the train back for his court appearance. So he did the most natural thing in the world – he stole a car. He forced its doors, and drove off with it to Liverpool. He then parked the stolen vehicle right outside the courts.

At the trial, a small miracle took place. Instead of imprisonment, the judge found David not guilty. He said the police had been harassing him and the case against him was unsound. David walked out of court a free man and in a state of absolute bliss. Fuck you, he thought to himself, fuck you.

Then he walked to his stolen car and found two policemen waiting for him.

'Is this vehicle yours?' one of the policemen asked. With a great big smile on his face.

David was handcuffed and led away.

'I suppose there's a moral in there somewhere,' he said.

'Yes, there is a moral,' I told David, 'and it's this – don't go to court in a stolen motor car and then park it outside in full view of the law.'

Both of us laughed and it felt good to be here with this man. Truth be told I had worried about the interview. I had worried the talk would go flat or horribly wrong. Just the opposite had occurred.

I was really enjoying my time with David Westbrook. Like Norman and me, we had twinned over care.

For the stolen car, David was remanded to Walton Prison, Liverpool. I couldn't imagine what that would be like. Prison scares me to my soul. In fact, I have nightmares about prison life.

'It was degrading,' David said. 'You're nothing. It made me feel that if I ever got out of there, I would never get caught again. I also felt that because of my past and because no one had ever given a shit about me, what I was doing was my way of getting back at society.'

David was released. With no job prospects in view and no one to guide him, he returned to crime and cheque fraud.

Yet the criminal's innate ability to know exactly when the net is closing in kicked into action. David sensed the law was getting closer so he bought a fake passport, hot footed it to St Tropez.

There he sold doughnuts on the beach and at night found himself in casual amorous adventures. He loved the day-to-day nature of this life, the freedom of waking up with just the day to think about.

But there was a shadow hanging over David and that shadow was the police. The constant worry of capture, he explained, was in itself a prison sentence. There was only one way to set himself free.

'I decided to give myself up,' he said. 'I got back from France and I phoned my probation officer. He said, "Come round and have a cup of tea." Ten minutes later two CID blokes who I knew arrived. One of them said to me, "We wondered where you had got to." I told him I had been in France but that enough was enough. I got remanded in custody.'

A change had taken place. Prison had initiated it, forced David to see, as that great poet Graham Parker once noted, that nobody hurts you harder than yourself.

David's solicitor did not mince words. He told David he would be imprisoned for a very long time. David shrugged his shoulders. 'I said, I know that,' he recalled, 'but at least I will have learnt my lesson.'

The court case came. Before sentencing, the magistrate asked David if he had anything to say.

'I stood up and I said, yes,' David said. 'I said, I have had a shit life. I have had people taking the piss out of me since I can remember, from the council to welfare to the police, but it is now time to go straight. I know you are going to send me away but I am telling you the truth, you won't see me again. I'm throwing the towel in.'

The magistrate retired to his room. When he returned he told David to stand. David stood. The magistrate gave David a chance, a last chance. He sentenced David to just twenty-eight days in prison. To David it was the most precious lifeline that had ever been given him.

'As we were leaving court,' David recalled, 'this CID bloke said to me, "You step in shit and you come out smelling of roses." Perhaps I said the right things, I told him. He said, "You'll be back again." I said, I won't. You will never ever see me again.'

And David was right. He spent twenty-eight days in Pentonville prison and was released. Immediately, he was re-arrested for other outstanding charges. But again his luck held. Another judge showed him beautiful mercy. Ellison was his name and David will never forget him.

'He didn't like me but he gave me a probation order which meant I had to live in a hostel in Guildford,' explains David. 'He said, I am going to ask the hostel for a report in three months' time and if I ever see you in here again you know what is going to happen.'

All orphans consider themselves unlucky. But once in a while the cards fall our way and when they do the impact feels so much greater than it does to others. Suddenly there is great light where there had only been dark and it feels absolutely wonderful.

David stayed in the hostel for a year, working for a national tyre service. He met a girl called Jackie, and they married. But there was dishonesty in the relationship. David was still closed off. How could he not be after a life that had left him full of shame, confusion and guilt – a man still unable to trust, carrying with him a huge fear of intimacy.

'Thing is, I never told anyone about my past,' he states. 'I felt ashamed, degraded, it wasn't the children's home thing it was more the criminal side of things. I couldn't talk to anyone about it. Same with Jackie, I didn't tell her anything.

'Of course she asked about my family, kept pestering me, so although I hadn't seen my foster dad for ages, in the end I went round there. I knocked on the door, he answered and I said, "Hello Dad." He said, "Blimey," and then the first thing he said to Jackie was, "He never comes to visit me." I thought, do you blame me? You've put me through shit. I really did resent him. He was my father and he had put me into care.'

And then it happened – David started crying. Not massively but tears appeared and flowed and his words stifled at the back of his throat. He asked me to turn off the tape recorder.

At first I was surprised. He had been so lively throughout the interview that I thought him in complete control of himself. But his dark recollections had taken him.

He had taken tremendous blows, been treated in the most terrible of ways, yet somehow he kept getting off the canvas and soldiering on. I know what it takes to do that. I know the price you have to pay.

And that is why I wanted to go over and hug David but the truth was I didn't know him well enough to do so.

All orphans are touch sensitive. Any display of emotion that has just one false note in it, sets our alarm bells ringing. If I had hugged him it would have been the act of a close friend, and I was not that to David.

It was best to leave him alone. To be false in any way would have seriously damaged the bond that had grown up between us.

I sat in my chair. But I could not help myself. I pushed out my hand across the table to him.

'David,' I said, 'it's fine, it's fine, all finished now, mate.'

'I'm sorry,' he said, using a tissue he had grabbed from the box on the shelf behind him. 'I didn't think I would crack.'

I told him we would stop the interview.

'No, no,' he insisted, 'nearly there now. I'm fine.'

He let out a sigh of ages, a sigh that said he that he was surprised at himself. He never suspected how deep the tears inside were.

David's marriage lasted seven years. Then his wife told him about the affair she had been having. End of marriage although there is a son, Dean, who he regularly sees.

He met Margaret in 1995 and just the mention of her name suddenly brightens him up. His smile reappears.

Margaret had no baggage. She was solid, someone of innate decency. Moreover, she offered him unconditional love. With Margaret, David would heal himself.

'Being married to Jackie I hated going home,' David said, 'With Margaret I hate leaving her. I never told Jackie anything about my past, whereas with Margaret I have told her everything.'

But why Margaret, why open up to her?

He thought about the question for a while.

'Because Margaret was open with me,' he said. 'I could talk to her about anything.'

In other words, the boy no one listened to had finally found someone who would listen.

'A lot of us who go through this get this drive to succeed,' David noted, 'and that's what Margaret helped find in me. She's my best friend. She's done so much for me.'

He vaguely gestured at his new expensive home, as if Margaret had built it for him. I suppose in many ways, she had.

'In 1996, I started my own air conditioning business. I worked really hard and I have made a big success of it. I've got so much today. I have got my freedom, I have got my sanity, I have a job, I earn really good money but best of all I have someone who cares for me, someone I trust implicitly. I can't ask for more.'

He smiled at me. I knew what that smile said. I reached over and turned off the tape recorder and then I smiled at him.

David smiled back and then he said, 'Thank you for listening.'

From: paolo@gmail.com
To: desh@hotmail.com
Subject: RE: RE: The New Book

Des – Hope all good. Went to see David Westbrook yesterday who I am sure you will remember. You will read about him in the book but suffice to say he is another one of us, someone who had to face problems and situations at far too early an age. At Burbank, just to get attention, he owned up to misdemeanours he did not commit. The result was that he was sent to Borstal and eventually did time in prison. But he is okay now, very much loved up that is for sure. Love in his case did indeed conquer all. It was lovely to see.

I wanted to tell you about this guy I hooked up with recently. His name is Sukhvinda. This mutual friend of ours works for this charity called the Bryn Meleyn group. I did a reading for them at the Houses of Parliament. Goldie the rapper and artist was there as well. He had time in care, as well. Basically, they try to help people who are having a tough time after leaving care. I mentioned to this girl, Janet, that I would be in Wolverhampton talking at a screening of the film *Get Carter* and she told me to meet up with a guy who had been in care. Really glad she did. This man had experienced the most horrendous times as a child. It is not right to reveal to you his background but Des I shiver when I think of what he went through. Yet you want to meet him. His energy and positive nature is uncontrollable and he was irresistible. I had to know, how had he got to a state so positive?

And he said this.

'Because Paolo, we orphans are the most important kids in the world.' The most important kids in the world, how good is that phrase, eh? I wanted to call this book that but had

to concede it didn't quite fit. But that's what we are and
always will be, mate. The Most Important Kids in the World.
Thought you should know that. I am around in about two
weeks' time. How are you fixed? And what about those
Spurs? Paolo

Four

Those the Gods Make Crazy

The Story of Terry Hodgson

He tried to kill me. With his fists. Bang, bang, bang. He said we were playing football in the garden and I had dribbled the ball past him just one too many times. That was when the red mist descended. That was when he knocked me to the ground, straddled me and started punching.

I would have been eleven years old, weighing eight stone. He would have been fourteen years old, weighing thirteen stone.

I would have put my arms against my head and turned to the right so as to protect my face. He would have kept pummelling away, slamming his huge fists into my face and prostrate body, time and time and time again.

But here's the thing, here's the knockout blow – I did not remember this savage beating at all. As soon as he gave me the details, I tried to access the event in my mind, but every time I did, nothing appeared.

It was not in my memory.

'But it's true,' Terry Hodgson insisted. 'I'll never forget it. I literally tried to kill you.'

'No, not me,' I said. 'You're thinking of someone else.'

'It was you.'

'No, it must have been another kid at Burbank.'

He shook his head. He was insistent.

'You. It was definitely you.'

'Are you sure?'

'Of course I am sure. God's honest. It is why I wanted to meet today.'

He looked at me, keenly.

'I wanted to say, sorry.'

He paused. 'I've been waiting to say sorry for years.'

Terry Hodgson looked up at me. We were sitting in a café in Woking Town. Coffee cups stood before us. Cake was on order. This was our home town and therefore felt appropriate, comfortable. Both our ghosts still lived in nearby Burbank and the road we once lived upon.

'Terry,' I said, 'if you did beat me like that, then – I forgive you, no problem.'

'Thank you,' he said. 'But I am surprised you can't remember this. Are you sure you can't? I remember that once I was upon you all the other kids in the garden ran over, and tried to pull me off. But my bulk made it impossible for them to shift me. Then I remember one of the kids ran up to the house and shouted for help and a staff member came running into the garden.'

That staff member also jumped onto Terry. No good. He could not pull Terry off me, either. Other staff appeared in the garden. They piled on top of him. In the end, it took three of them to stop Terry beating the hell out of me.

'And I am sure you went to hospital,' he insisted. 'That is how bad I had beaten you.'

'No,' I said. 'I'd remember that.'

'Are you sure?' Terry asked.

'I remember all my hospital visits,' I said. 'At Burbank, I had just the one. Sprained my wrist, playing football.'

'Well, it is true,' he said, 'true as I am sitting here.'

After being pulled away from me, Terry was taken up to the house, put in an empty room. The door was shut on him. He paced the room. Clouds of red gripped his mind. Fury mixed with chaos. Madness, madness, madness.

'I just hated myself,' he said. 'I didn't know what the fuck was going on. I just knew I was fucking mad,' he recalled.

He tried the door. The door opened. He came out into the corridor. No one was around. He turned left, went through the back door and was outside the house.

He walked quickly around Burbank and then went down the drive. A quick right, and then a quick left, and he was free and headed for town, Woking town.

He reached the outskirts of the train station, climbed a fence and then scrambled up onto the railway tracks. His breath was now deep and irregular. He walked alongside the tracks until he came to a bridge.

He stopped, looked down. Cars shot by beneath him. Whoosh – whoosh – whoosh. Good place to end it all, he thought to himself.

'And I was just about to jump onto the road, just about to kill myself, because I knew I was mad,' Terry said matter of factly, 'when I heard someone shout behind me, and I turned round and all these fucking coppers are legging it across the tracks towards me and I thought "Fuck this!" and I jumped back over the side and I started legging it too.

'They got me and they put me in a police car and took me straight up to Brookwood Hospital. When I got to Brookwood they put me in a padded cell, gave me an injection and put me to sleep for three days. I never came back to Burbank.'

* * *

Terry today: still big but not fat. Suited, tie a little askew, nervous, lights dancing occasionally across his eyes. Quick talker, laughs a lot, a little too much laughter. Maybe. Smokes. A lot. Tells me his memory is shot through constant abuse of drink and drugs.

Example: Goes into a coffee shop for a sandwich, is asked what he would like? He freezes. Can't remember. Goes outside and it hits him. I want a sandwich. That is what I want. He goes back in and says to the man, 'A sandwich, please.' And the man says, 'What kind, sir?'

Fuck, now you're asking.

It is apposite that he mentioned drugs. After our meeting, I would liken the telling of his story to a surreal drug experience. Reader, best fasten your seat belt. You are about to take a massive trip.

The first day I met Terry Hodgson I was on an introductory visit to Burbank. I was ten years old, shot through with fear and apprehension. I was walking down the curved pathway to the left of the house when I came across Terry and another boy digging a ditch.

Terry stopped what he was doing, looked at me, and then stabbed his pick-axe towards me.

'Oi new boy, I am going to put this in your fucking head,' he said.

I quickly walked off and vowed never to go near him again. His anger scared and then confused me.

But then, how could I know that three years previously he had been rejected in one of the most callous manners I had ever heard.

The rejection came in the form of a letter, a letter which would cause such anguish, turbulence, pain and violence, create so many tears and so much heartbreak, it was staggering.

Words on paper.

Words on paper.

That letter pushed Terry Hodgson into a life of such crazy turbulence that it took the intervention of God Himself to restore his sanity.

The early facts are clear enough. Terry Hodgson was born on 6th June 1955. His father was not his mother's husband. Naughty girl, Mrs Hodgson, you let your knickers down. Divorce and scandal followed.

Terry and his mother went to live in a mother and baby home. These institutions keep popping up in this book. And the world spins round.

The mother despised life under disapproving inspection. One day, she walked, walked out of the Home, and never returned. Terry was two years old.

God only knows what damage it caused within. Never mind, much more to follow. Give us another hit, Tel.

A local family came to visit, offered to foster him. Today, Terry believed their motives suspicious, thought that the mother needed something to take her mind off things at home.

Many foster parents wanted children for the money or simply to take revenge for their own harsh childhood.

Like my foster mother. She beat me because someone beat her. And so the world spins round.

'My foster mother had two children of her own and she couldn't have any more,' Terry said. 'She wanted a plaything not a baby.'

Terry told me his foster mother was 'a very kind, warm-hearted woman but she was totally dominated by her husband.'

The dad, well, what a bastard. Beat Terry as soon as he could lay his hands on him.

Example: Family go shopping. Terry gets in the car, instantly he gets sick. Father's reaction? Beat the boy.

Tell me about it. Had the same with my foster mother. I used to clamber into her car with those dark brown leather seats and within five minutes I would be retching.

Any love and sympathy from my guardian? Any hugs, any encouraging words to cure my sickness? Hell, no. Just a smack around the face, a smack around the head, and no pocket money for a week.

There was only one person Terry could run to, his foster grandfather. Listen to the excitement and the love in Terry's words as his saviour comes to mind.

'We used to go fishing together, we used to walk in the woods, we used to do everything together,' Terry said.

'He used to sneak me pocket money because my foster parents never gave me anything. He used to take me for rides on his motorbike over the woods; oh we had a fantastic time, me and him. He was a really nice old guy, he was how a grandad should be, the sort of grandad I try to be, he was a good man. It was a shame when he died. He was a painter and decorator all of his life and, when he was about sixty, he had to retire because his hips gave in. He lived to eighty-three, he smoked every day of his life.'

Terry was safe with this man. Time spent with him was a time where no one screamed at him or punched him, or brought him to his knees in humiliation.

How then could the father be so different to the son, one so kind and caring, the other so cruel and unforgiving? How can two joined by blood differ so wildly?

I ask because I faced exactly the same conundrum in my childhood. My foster mother was vicious and vindictive, rarely kind or giving. Her mother, a paragon of kindness and gentleness.

It is the anomaly that consistently puzzles.

'I couldn't do anything right,' Terry said of his foster father. 'I don't recall him ever saying to me "Well done." Grandad could say it, he could see the value in me. He used to say, well done. But my foster dad…I used to suffer from asthma and I remember once I had a bad attack late at night, and I opened the bedroom window.

'The only way I could bloody survive was to lean out of the window getting my breath, he came in and he belted me for it. He didn't say "What you doing? What's going on?" He screamed "Shut that fucking window!" And then he hit me.'

Such hatred, such cruelty, and why?

Because father was no longer the centre of attention. Terry had taken his place. Therefore, Terry must be removed.

His plan was devious, crafty. It would cost him money but the way he saw it, it would be worth every penny.

He would send Terry to a boarding school in Dorset. A phone call was made. Terry's suitcase was packed. The uncomprehending boy was taken to the station and put on a train.

Dad went home exultant: he was again numero uno in the family.

But there was a flaw to the plan, a turn of events the father had overlooked. It was Terry. He could not settle at his new school. How could he? Damage had been done to his soul. He was too unhappy. Too scared. Too fearful.

He kept playing up. With teachers, with the police, with his class mates, anyone, in fact, that he came into contact with. All were fair game.

Back home, family life was constantly interrupted by phone calls from authority figures telling of Terry's wayward behaviour.

'I would go to boarding school and get into trouble with the police all the time,' Terry said,

'The final thing was breaking into a quarry and driving a big bulldozer over the edge of a cliff, kid's stuff, vandalism, you know what I mean?'

I didn't. Know what he meant, that is. A smashed bus stop was the closest I ever got to vandalism. And it wasn't even me who did it, guv. It was Den Harvey.

It kind of pales a bit in front of sending a bulldozer flying over a cliff.

Terry was moved to another school, and then another, and then another.

Their names became a blur, so did the memories. Terry continually ran away, continually caused trouble. Eventually, he ended up at a school in Wishmore Cross, near Camberley, Surrey.

Meanwhile, the father sat at home and listened to the daily calls of complaints against Terry and he thought to himself, will no one rid me of this turbulent child?

Finally, his brooding turned to action. He reached for pen and paper.

The most significant day of Terry Hodgson's life had just dawned.

Words on paper.
Words on paper.

It was morning, a bright morning, sunny, bluish skies. Summer was fading, autumn approached. Yellow and brown leaves were readying themselves for the fall.

Terry was in art class and his mind was elsewhere when his teacher came over and handed him a letter.

'We weren't supposed to read letters there and then,' he said, 'but I opened my letter and I read it and I went into a state of shock. It was from my foster father and it said, we don't want you to come home anymore, you're not our child, you're not one of us.'

Silence, there was silence between us. The only sound was that of Woking itself, of hurried cars and busy shoppers, trains that rumbled into platforms, the odd wave of breathless conversation passing us by, the sound of a twenty-first century British town seeking to pass another day without damage.

All around us, people completely oblivious to what had just been revealed.

Which is that Terry Hodgson had been completely and utterly discarded by his family. They had thrown him away. Like a sack of rubbish, like dirt-stained and unwanted leaves, stuffed into a bag and thrown into the world.

The father could not stomach his presence anymore so he had done what he had wanted to do for a long time. He had banished Terry from his world.

Now, Terry had nothing, literally nothing. No family, no home, no parents, no anything.

And he is ten years old.

'And I read the letter and I read it and I read it, and I remember the art teacher coming to me... I think people realised something was wrong. I could sense everybody knew there was something wrong.'

The art teacher took Terry by the arm and led him into the kiln room.

'He just left me there with the letter. And then I blew my stack. I smashed every bit of pottery in there. Then I walked out and went and sat in the middle of the playing fields.'

In that field, in that lonely expanse of grass, the ten-year-old Terry placed an imaginary fifty yard radius circle around him and determined to attack anyone who stepped over that invisible line.

If you really want to know what the orphan feels like, if you ever want to get close to the orphan soul, then I can think of no better image to give you than that of Terry, sat in a field, utterly alone, baffled and discombobulated, denied the very stuff of life – family, love, comfort, security, want, birth right.

And not just Terry either – every orphan has had to sit in that field and make that circle at some point in their lives.

Two teachers approached him. Don't come any nearer, Terry warned them. But they persisted. So like a snarling dog he flew at them and they ran for their lives.

Then some of his class mates approached him. Same result. They got close, Terry attacked, and they too, ran for their lives.

'They banned all the kids,' Terry said. 'Kids weren't allowed out of school and they just left me to it. Then, after four days, the headmaster came to see me. Now, I can't tell you how fantastic our headmaster was...'

'Four days?' I asked. 'Four days? You were sleeping there, as well?'

'Yes.'

'You stayed in that field for four days solid?'

'Yes.'

'You didn't eat, drink?'

'I would get up to stretch my legs and just walk around the field. When I wanted a piss I used to just walk a bit away from where I was sitting, and piss on the field, then go and sit back down again. I stayed there night and day for four days.'

'No blankets?'

'No, nothing.'

'Was this during the summer?'

'It was September or the beginning of October.'

'It was cold?'

'Yeah, but I didn't notice any of that, I didn't notice nothing, I was just sitting there and a fifty yard radius was my space and anybody entered my space they died.'

'But four days?'

I shook my head in disbelief. By now, I should have been immune to such awful events unravelling themselves into my tape recorder but this was something else.

'Anyway this headmaster came over, and he was such a wonderful guy. He walked towards me very slowly, very unthreateningly, and he sat down, I don't know five yards... ten yards away, and he just sat there cross-legged. He didn't try to speak, he didn't say a word to me, he just sat there.

'I don't know if I realised it at the time or if it's just looking back, but now I know exactly what he was doing, he was getting on my wavelength. We've all got psychic levels and we can adjust to where each other are at and that's exactly what he did with me.

'He sat there until he felt he was at my level, and then he said to me, "What's going on, Terry?" I said, "I got a letter from home." He said, "Do you want to show me?" I said, "Yeah, sure," I gave it to him.

'If I remember rightly, it was just two sheets of ordinary letter paper this letter and it took him half an hour to read it, I think he went through exactly what I went through. He just said to me "I'm so sorry, Terry," and I said something like "Yeah, well," and he said, "I had no idea about this, we never knew anything," and then he started crying. I can't remember exactly what he said but it was something like "I'll leave you to it," he just got up and walked away.

'The next morning, I think it was the next morning, I got up. I went back to the school, helped myself to some breakfast.'

Not long after, Terry assaulted his science teacher, and was called into his headmaster's study. The head teacher said, 'Terry, we can't take any more of this; it's got to stop now.'

'And he picked up his cane and he said, "Bend over the desk," and these were the days of six of the best. But instead I took the cane off him and I beat him with it, I wasn't having any of that shit. And then I got expelled from there.'

He paused for comic effect. 'They've got no sense of humour these people.'

There was nowhere else for Terry Hodgson to go now, except into care, carrying a voice which incessantly told him: *You are not wanted, you are not wanted, you are not wanted.*

Words on paper.

Words on paper.

* * *

Terry entered care, a wounded, angry, rejected animal, the raging bull.

Carrying a physique beyond his years, Terry roared at everyone. And everyone backed off. Blessed are the angry for they shall inherit the Children's Home.

'I am going to put this pick-axe in your fucking head.'

Terry was sent to the nearby Byfleet Secondary School but said he got expelled within a few days. For smashing windows.

'I got done for thieving, shoplifting in Guildford and the Wych Hill Post Office.' (Burbank is on Wych Hill.) 'And I was always being brought back by the police, or Barry was having to rescue me, that was happening a hell of a lot.

'When I first went to Burbank,' Terry remembered, 'there was someone who ran it and I'm sure his name was Board, Donald Board. Then he left and Barry and Julie came. Donald Board was like an administrative head of the Home whereas I always saw Barry and Julie as a mum and dad in a way. That was the difference between them, Barry and Julie really took an interest, that sort of thing, I liked them a lot, I really liked them.'

Still, didn't stop him smoking, and stealing and trying to get others to follow his example. Me, for instance.

After the pick-axe incident I had won Terry's grudging respect one memorable day by climbing on a bicycle and pulling off a dangerous stunt.

Now, I went with Terry to the boiler room for a smoke.

He asked, I followed.

All of his orders I obeyed. Yet he was not a bully. Not like Mothy who beat me senseless for a year.

Certainly, Terry was ready to explode, potentially dangerous, but I don't remember him as cruel.

Threatening, yes. Scary, yes.

But not cruel. He told me his first feelings when he calmed down after the beating he administered upon me, were those of huge regret.

'I liked you,' he told me plainly, 'I liked you a lot. The fact that I had attacked you really upset me. That is one of the reasons why I wanted to kill myself. I thought, how could I do that to him?'

And that was why on the day I can't remember Terry Hodgson was admitted to Brookwood psychiatric hospital.

Because he wanted to kill himself. Over me.

'Wasn't the late comedian Spike Milligan a patient there?' I asked Terry. I was trying to break the mood. I knew about Brookwood hospital. It was the building on the outskirts of Woking.

Like Burbank, it was hidden from view.

'Yes, and Russ Conway was there,' Terry said. 'I met him in there. It was like that film, *One Flew Over the Cuckoo's Nest* that was how it was. There were people in there frothing at the mouth, stamping on the floor, banging their heads, all this kind of stuff. And I was sitting there thinking, "I'm not one of these."

'Eventually I managed to work my way out, I got cleaning jobs, I used to sweep the roads at the hospital. Within about three months I was running the social club.'

'I started off setting up tables,' he explained. 'They used to have bingo and tea dances and I used to set that up. And then I used to use the social club as an excuse for going out on the town, and I joined a group of Hells Angels who were based up at Knaphill. What was the name of that café? The Copper Kettle, we used to meet at the Copper Kettle.'

I had lived in Woking for eight years and had never heard of any Hells Angels in the area. So two days after my meet, I called my mate Pete G. His family home was a mile from Knaphill.

'Pete, Hells Angels. Round your way. True or not?'

'Nah,' Pete said, 'Never heard of them. Not round here.'

I smiled. Bullshitter, Terry. That is what I will call you from now on. Bullshitter Terry.

A day later, Pete was back on the phone. 'Mentioned your question to my mate at work. He is local as well and he said there definitely was a bunch of bikers round there in the seventies. Used to hang out at a café called the Copper Kettle.'

Terry was a biker, a Hells Angel. I stood corrected. And a little shameful.

Terry stayed with the gang for a few months. But as time passed, his enthusiasm dimmed. Ironically, an act of violence did for him. One day, they forced him to beat an innocent kid up. The act made him feel sick to his soul.

'I used to intimidate people but that was all,' Terry recalls. 'One day we were all driving along and there was this couple there and someone shouted something at them and the bloke responded, wrong thing to do. I was on the back of the leader's bike and he said to me, "Right, this is it, do the business."

'So I got off the bike and went up to the bloke and I gave him a pasting, and I hated it. I was into anger, I was into destroying the world. I hated the world, but I couldn't do it cold-bloodedly, I had to be mad, something had to upset me.'

Funny that: the boy who screamed in anger at the world was the boy who shirked the fight.

Brookwood hospital looked after the old as well as the young. The authorities decided to move Terry to a more youth orientated hospital, Farmstead Villa in Epsom, Surrey.

Terry remembered his time at Farmstead well, always will do. It was here he first experienced marijuana and LSD. He greedily took to them. Who wouldn't? They altered your world, made it a different and better place. Sometimes. Other times, the drugs unleashed dark enormous powers, well beyond his control.

'Once I nearly jumped off a multi-storey car park trying to catch aeroplanes,' he said. 'Other times I would have frightening trips where everything would go black and white.'

At Farnstead, Terry hooked up with a guy called Chris. They not only took drugs, they stole drugs, and then they stole money to buy drugs.

At night, he got high and touched the sky but one nightmare refused to go away: the letter, the letter, everything revolved around that letter.

Everything gained momentum from that letter, the letter that told Terry Hodgson he was not needed or loved or wanted. It is the letter that sent him crazy.

You are not wanted, you are not wanted.

Words on paper.

Words on paper.

When Terry reached sixteen years of age he had to leave Farmstead. Those were the rules, my friend. So he joined the armed forces. Lots of care kids do. The world is too large, too scary to cope with. The forces shield you from civilian life. You serve, they protect. It's a good deal.

Terry went to a Merchant Navy training school based in Arundel, Kent, got assigned to a ship called The Bembridge. One night on duty he got drunk, thought the ship was on fire and hit the alarm. Everyone jumped into the water. False alarm. The smoke Terry had seen was steam from a boiler room.

Terry was discharged, moved back to Woking. He found a job at Tesco's but he was too out of control. No one could tell him what to do, where to go.

Tesco's sacked Terry. So he did what all sacked employees do. He set light to the store. In his mind, he was the singer Arthur Brown shouting, 'Fire! I'll leave you to burn!' at all his enemies.

Then he got a job at Superdrug across the road on Woking High Street. Again, he was sacked. So he set light to Superdrug as well, and then hotfooted it down to Bath, where he began another campaign of revenge.

This time, it was against his foster family.

He called the local undertakers, told them that his father had died and gave the house address. He asked could they please come round with a coffin. Imagine the father's face when he opened the door. 'Come to bury you, sir.'

One night, high on LSD in Bath, he came across a burger van. He bought eight pounds worth of burgers and spent the night chucking them at passing cars, laughing hysterically.

'I was mad at the world,' he said. Others disagreed. They said, Terry Hodgson is mad in this world.

He left Bath, and went back to Woking. He stepped onto the High Street, the boulevard of my teenage dreams, and was promptly arrested for arson.

Tesco's and Superdrug, they do not forget. Or forgive.

He was put on remand at Ashford Centre. Then he was taken to court. The judge was told that Terry was borderline insane.

He remembered a big row then going on in the court between doctors from two hospitals, one of which was Broadmoor.

'They all wanted me,' he drily noted.

He was given a bed in a hospital called Longrove, in Epsom, Surrey. He did not stay long. Soon, he had escaped and was on the run.

He got a job at a fruit and veg wholesaler. At the interview, Terry said yes, I can drive a fork-lift. The first time they asked him to drive a fork-lift he puts its spears through the side of his manager's car.

'Then I got a job at a petrol station, on the night shift. It was all right, I was relatively normal. But I got pissed off, so one night I took all the takings and pissed off. This was about one o'clock in the morning. I filled up my car with petrol,

I shut up shop and I hit the road. The next morning I hit upon a brilliant scheme.

'I ring the police and in an Irish accent tell them that I am the IRA and that we have kidnapped a Terry Hodgson from a service station near Sheffield and unless they release the Price sisters he will be executed.'

(Marian and Dolours Price were part of a unit that placed four car bombs in London on 8th March 1973 and were subsequently imprisoned.)

'I waited a bit and then I called them back. I told them the Price sisters were not free, therefore Terry Hodgson was dead. We, the IRA, had murdered him. Goodbye.'

Now that he was dead, Terry assumed the identity of a criminal he knew to have disappeared. He carried on stealing and robbing. His chaos was at work and in full flight. Eventually, he was caught and he went to court. At his trial, the IRA scam was revealed. Terry got off with a suspended sentence.

'And I got a great headline in the local paper,' he said.

'What was it?' I asked.

'IRA Killed Me Said Thief,' he replied.

Both of us dissolved into waves of laughter.

* * *

His was now a life of utter abandonment. There was no control, no boundaries. The world had rejected him and so Terry created a life without top or bottom to it, one without any sides. He had no future, no direction, just anger and criminality, and making sure he threw back at the world what it had thrown at him.

His violence was one long scream.

He ended up in Dover and appropriated a car. He ran, he schemed, he stole. It was all madness; a life lived in an endless whirlwind of cops against Terry, Terry against the world, Terry against himself.

You are not wanted, you are not wanted.

Finally, he was committed to Broadmoor psychiatric hospital. Broadmoor. Reggie Kray was a fellow inmate, so was Peter Sutcliffe the Yorkshire Ripper.

How did he survive, I wondered.

'I pulled the poor, hard-done-by number on the doctors there.'

I instantly understood.

'The poor little me you can't punish me routine?' I asked.

He nodded and we both smiled, conspiratorially. All orphans used this trick. I used mine at school.

If a teacher started telling me off I would count to three and then interject. 'Yes sir,' I would say, 'but in the Children's Home I live in…' and instantly they would pull up, and say 'Well, don't do it again,' and walk off and forget to punish me. I would turn and smile and skip away.

Terry was careful at Broadmoor. Compared to his inmates, he was the sane one. In Broadmoor, he told me, matter of fact, he saw people raped and killed. So he kept his distance, befriended no one, tried to sink into the surroundings and not be noticed.

'There were people in there that I could have had sex with but you wouldn't risk it, because there was a good chance that while you were shagging or whatever they'd put a knife in your back. So, I played the game and I got out. But to show you how mad I was, I'd been out six months and then I went back and pleaded to go back in. I wanted to go back. I hated the outside world at first; it was such hard grind living in central London.'

They would not let Terry back into Broadmoor, so he headed for London, ended up in a Richmond Fellowship hostel. Ladbroke Grove. It was here he became a professional villain.

His scams were devious, and clever. He told me one of them.

Terry bought a Cortina Crusader car and advertised it in the local paper. He sold the car and told his client that as soon as the cheque was cleared he would hand over the car. An hour later another man calls. Car advertised still available?

Yes sir. More men come and hand over cheques. He banks all the cheques, and, after three days, he ran off with the money.

What does he spend his De Niro on? What else? Women, wine and song, of course. What else is there in life?

Terry turned gangster, began acting the big shot. You know the number. You've seen the films. Get yourself smart, get yourself a gang, get yourself some money, drive the big car, and here come the girls.

Terry moved to Eastbourne and earnt eight hundred quid a day. Fraud, mainly. At night, he partied. He went to nightclubs, slipped doormen wads of notes, ordered bottle after bottle of the good stuff, and the girls came and sat with him.

'It was the crack you know? Made me feel good.'

I would never have been so flash. My life in care drove me to stand on the side-lines, watch others. Terry's impulse drove him centre stage, into the spotlight. Look at me, I am the one.

The police get interested in this Flash Harry. Terry ended up in a car chase.

A day later Terry Hodgson woke up in Lewes Prison.

'And that was when I met God,' he said, casually.

'How is He?' I asked, facetiously.

Terry considered me carefully. 'Do you believe?' he said.

'Forgive the smart ass remark. I do,' I said.

'I'm sitting in my cell and I'm a hard man, I'm known in that prison and there are people out to get me. So I'm sitting in there and I suddenly said, "God, you know, if you're real you gonna have to prove yourself to me now because I am in deep shit." And He did. He spoke to me, I heard words in my head.'

'What did He say?'

'He said, "Terry, I've been here all the time and I am ready to help you, just believe in me, just trust in me." And I said to him, "You know my reputation, there are people here who are going to give me grief if I believe in you, they're gonna think I've gone soft and they're gonna get me." And he showed me a verse in the Bible. I just opened a Bible and there was this verse that said, "I will give trouble to those that trouble you." And I just knew in my heart that this was right and I went for it, and I had a great time.'

Terry thought this act was preparing him for the next step. Which was miraculous. He was set free from court. He did not serve a prison sentence.

'God had been true to his word,' Terry said.

I have already sensed your uneasiness, reader, your discomfort. I understand. Mention of God, suspicious eh? The idea that He might be directly helping people is too much for the many to bear.

Did God speak to Terry Hodgson, as he claims, or did Terry simply find some kind of peace through the idea of a God talking directly to him, around him for so many years?

This must be said, though.

Since that day in 1982, Terry Hodgson did not commit any more crimes. Not one. Instead he dedicated his life to God. God the Father, God the Son, God the Holy Spirit.

As a free man, he regularly attended mass. He began a website where he posted his musings on the subject and later on bought a printing company so he could publish Christian magazines. The business failed. He went to work for a bookseller, then onto driving the lorries.

The personal life has not been smooth, either. In 1984 he married a woman named Ginny and had two daughters. In 1999 his marriage fell apart but in keeping with his new outlook he and Ginny remained friends.

Later on, he suffered a heart attack and was told he had just six months to live. By now he was in with a woman named Claire and she was the one, the love he sought. They decided to move down to Devon so they could be with his daughters for the last part of his life.

'I started going to a hospital for tests and treatments and on the first day,' Terry said, 'they turned round to me and said, "What do you mean dying? There's nothing wrong with you, you've got the heart of an ox." I said, "What do you mean? I've just given up a perfectly good life in Surrey to move down here." So, there's nothing wrong with me and I haven't had any trouble since.'

The couple stayed on in Devon. Then, disaster. Claire fell ill, was diagnosed with benign inter-cranial hypertension.

'It's a brain disease, it's to do with epilepsy. When's she at her worst she really believes she is fourteen years old,' Terry said. 'Other times she'll just sleep for days, sometimes she just wanders around, doesn't see me, doesn't know me, doesn't see anything, just on automatic.'

'Must be so very difficult for you.'

'It's very difficult, thoughts of suicide are a constant companion,' he admitted.

'For you or for her?'

'For me, it can be very depressing, I never will, mainly because I haven't got the gun. But I just get through, when I get a run of my really bad depressions I just turn round and say: tomorrow's another day.'

Which seemed as good a place as any to leave it.

I was exhausted. Terry's life had been so rich, so adventurous I needed a day just to assimilate it all. He walked me back to the station.

'By the way,' he said, as we parted, 'don't get me too wrong on this God thing. This geezer took the piss the other day and I did have to threaten him with a little slap.'

And the boy who once sat alone in a field for four days and the man he came close to killing, both laughed together.

And then we both slowly faded upwards into the early evening sky, high on the trip we had just taken.

From: paolo@gmail.com

To: desha@hotmail.com

Subject: RE: RE: RE: The New Book

Des – Hope all well. Last week met up with Terry Hodgson, Jesus that was some day. His life was absolutely crazy. Parts I did not believe but then I checked some of his story and it came out true. And he seems all right now. God saved him. His life was crazy and chaotic and then he called on God and the madness stopped. I know where you stand on this matter but even if God does not exist is that not a fantastic reason for His existence? That there is a force where just the *idea* of Him is enough to turn people's lives around for the better. Today I am off to see my sister in Yeovil so better shoot. How you getting on with *The Sopranos*? Talk soon. x

Things Seen at Dawn

God's breath is the early morning mist that gently invades the Somerset hills. At the bottom of those hills begins a carpet of green that slowly undulates itself towards me.

The sky is an unblemished blue, the sun is a yellow ball slowly breathing itself into heat, second by second and minute by minute.

It is seven in the morning and I am sitting in my sister Nina's garden sipping espresso and thinking about the poet, Shelley. Was it not he who said that heaven is here on earth, that the curse of our existence is that we are just too blind to see it?

I want to shake the man's hand. If the view in front of me was made beautiful by one more inch I don't think I could stand it.

Everything is so right, so perfect, so tranquil.

Van Morrison now appears in front of me, singing that beautiful song of his about the angels that live in the land just across the bridge, and how to see them I must close my eyes.

So I close my eyes and I wonder and I dream yet I feel a slight disquiet in my soul. I know the problem.

Even though I am having a relaxing weekend I cannot help thinking about this book. I go to bed at night with it on my mind, I wake up in the morning thinking on it. It is a familiar set of instructions.

Don't forget to insert that sentence, don't forget to resolve that issue, don't forget to introduce that character, make sure you write Terry's in a fractured style so as to reflect a drug trip, keep this section in the present tense so as to insert some energy, and – most important of all – think up a great opening line for the next section, one that grabs the reader and won't let them go.

Also keep Norman's chapter terse, so as to reflect his character on the road and the same with David so as to mirror the frustration of a child that no one listens to.

Although I have now interviewed the four guys and written their chapters, there is something missing, someone I have not met and faced up to. First off, I think it must be that I have not spoken to any of the girls who I lived with.

There is an explanation for this anomaly. I found two girls from my Burbank days, and both refused to talk. They had no interest in telling their life stories. When they told me their reasons, I understood why.

So if it wasn't the girls…

And then, a beautiful realisation.

Burbank Children's Home. That is the character missing from this book, the character that binds us all together. Burbank Children's Home.

Many years ago in my memoir, *The Looked After Kid* I described Mount Vesuvius in the bay of Naples as a brooding, imperious presence. I think I was actually describing Burbank.

For so many years, that is exactly what it has been at the back of my mind.

When I moved to London, I did so because I wanted to escape its dark shadows, its ghosts, its bitter sweet memories. I wanted to forget I was an orphan, escape from that title and re-invent myself.

At first, I told no one of my past in London. My aim was to write for the music press and I did not want to achieve that dream by playing the sympathy vote. I wanted to be judged fair and square.

Of course, when I did land my dream job, I became convinced that my employers IPC had a huge secret computer stashed away somewhere which had given them my details and that is why I had been given the job.

Let us put that thought aside. The reality is this – I need, no, have to meet Burbank, and face it head on. I *have to* visit every one of its rooms and dispel forever this dark presence in my soul.

The wheel has turned, the bell has rung: I have no choice now. It is time to face Burbank full on. And I knew just the man to do it with.

I reach for my phone and I call him.

'You are coming to Burbank with me and you can't say no,' I say, and then I hang up.

Happy as the morning sun now, I took some more coffee, closed my eyes and lost myself in those fields of wonder.

Five

Home

Inside Burbank a million of my ghosts lived and breathed. Today, I must go inside, firmly shake their hands and bid them *addio* forever.

I had actually visited Burbank once before but I had TV cameras following me. We had three hours to film and so I had quickly moved through its rooms, refused to engage with my ghosts.

Today, I will go eye to eye with them. Today, I have to.

As I waited nervously for Des Hurrion, a plane passed above me and I looked upwards. It was June and I saw that God had awoken in an uncertain mood. Thin grey clouds stretched themselves thinly across a sky blue canvas as if He couldn't make up his mind between sun and rain.

The air's temperature fluctuated, hot and cold, cold and hot.

The arrangement was to meet each other at Woking train station at ten in the morning and take a leisurely stroll to the Home. Only I got there late and Des was nowhere to be seen. I figured he had already made his way to Burbank and I set off in pursuit.

Fifteen minutes I later I turned into the drive that led up to the Home and received my first jolt of the day. The garden that stood to the right of the drive, the garden I had spent so much of my time in, was no longer there.

Two massive houses now stood in that space. They cost half a million each.

The hallowed ground I had spent countless hours upon as I played football, smoked ciggies, chased girls, fought other boys, was now covered by bricks and mortar.

I felt a surge of hopelessness, and a tinge of anger. My teenage spirit was soaked in that soil. Now the foundations of my youth were the foundations of two strangers' homes.

It felt terribly wrong.

I continued up the drive and suddenly Burbank came into view. I stopped, looked. Still the same colour, still the same structure. I had heard rumours in faraway London that there had been plans to knock it down and even though I had spent many years running from its presence, the very idea of its disappearance had been strong enough to induce in me a faint kind of panic.

Now, I knew better. It had not changed one iota. This house will stand forever.

I reached the porch and rang a bell. The front door opened. A young staff member called Gary stood in front of me. He had blond hair, a good build.

'You're Paolo?'

'I am.'

'Des was here but he's gone looking for you,' Gary informed me.

'I'll wait for him out here,' I said. 'Don't worry, I'll be fine.'

I was doing Gary a slight favour here. These days, there are strict rules and regulations concerning visits to a children's home. You have to be accompanied by a staff member at all times. As Des wasn't with me Gary didn't know whether to invite me in or ask me to wait outside.

I had just saved him from having to make that awkward decision.

He closed the door and I waited to meet my past. It felt strange to loiter by the front door. During my time at Burbank, as you may recall from Norman's testimony, the front door was only used for special occasions.

Mine was the day the police picked me up at school and drove me back to Burbank after burgling Woking Football Club.

I remember Barry waiting for me by this very front door. He wore lime green socks with no shoes, and the expression of rage on his face was fearsome.

Those lime green socks were the colour of my fear.

'There you are!'

I looked down the drive and saw Des.

With blokish irony, I shouted, 'Oi! Come on, Hurrion! Where've you been?'

'Waiting for you, you plonker,' he chided back. And in that very moment we suddenly stood glorious again in 1972, transported there by our words, our pact, the language of our bodies.

Today, Des looked great. The man had a smile on his lips and air in his steps. His face was beaming and his enthusiasm obvious. He had lived in so many places since leaving Burbank but had settled in Guildford, the town he loved. And it showed.

'Look at what they have done to our garden,' I said, motioning to the two houses. 'I learnt to play football on that grass.'

'Were you any good?' he cheekily asked.

'Better than you my friend,' I shot back.

'Yeah right,' he said.

Both of us looked down the drive.

'Do you remember the phone hoaxes that someone used to make once in a while?' Des unexpectedly asked. 'I think one of the kids had left the Home and would ring the fire brigade and tell them Burbank was on fire.

'I'll always remember fleets of fire engines roaring up this drive to put out non-existent fires. In fact one time Barry had to wrest an axe from an over-zealous fireman who was about to smash his way through the front door.'

'I wonder who made those calls,' I said.

'I remember Barry said the name of some kid I had never heard of,' Des replied.

'Wouldn't be a Terry Hodgson by any chance?'

'Could well be,' Des said.

'I also remember finding the house dog, Shandy, dead on this very porch we are standing on,' Des said with a small laugh, 'and me and Barry hurriedly rushing to bury it in the grounds before anyone got home from school.'

'You buried the dog?'

'Yeah, round the side there, in the slope leading down to the road. Barry and I did it one afternoon. I remember we were really rushing because everyone was going to be home from school soon so we had to get it done before you guys got back and got very upset.'

'Jesus.'

Five minutes in and already dark secrets are being revealed.

Gary opened the door.

'Come in,' he said warmly to both of us, 'Come on in.'

We walked into the house, into the hallway, and now we stood on the familiar mosaic floor we had trodden so many times as child orphans, and I could not help but be taken by this moment.

When I arrived at Burbank in August of 1968, I was a young boy, full of so much fear and confusion that I didn't know I was full of so much fear and confusion.

I stood in this very hallway with a small suitcase in my hand, not knowing what to do, what to say, where to go. Now, I stood here, a grown man with purpose in my soul.

Instinctively, I looked over to the right hand corner of the hallway. That's where Barry once placed a dog bowl in which he had mixed my cigarettes with water. He had caught me smoking and was determined to make an example of me in front of everyone.

'You love cigarettes so much,' he cried to me, 'drink that.'

This from a man who smoked forty a day. In front of us.

Gary said, 'You understand I have to accompany you everywhere? I hope you don't mind but it's the law.'

Des and I had no problem with this.

'Actually, I am looking forward to this,' Gary added.

Care had changed so much since our time there, Gary explained, and he wanted to measure the distances between then and now, see how far care had come.

I liked the man's dedication.

Des turned to Gary. 'How many children now live here?' he asked.

The number of children during our time at Burbank oscillated between twenty to twenty-five. Barry and Julie ran the Home and lived with us along with one other live-in staff member. Two other staff came in daily from outside.

Today, Gary told us, Burbank had just three children with five staff to look after them.

'What?!' we both exclaimed.

'Five staff, three children. That's the numbers,' he replied. 'Different times now.'

'Certainly are,' I said. 'Did you see that TV programme the other night about care in Germany?' I asked. 'The kids there get massages every week.'

'The kids here get one-on-one counselling,' Gary said.

'We could have done with some of that,' Des softly noted.

'I know,' I say, 'but let's face facts. The staff had enough on their hands getting twenty-five of us clothed, fed and watered every day. They had to get us to school and back, make sure the house was in order, provide food and then get us to bed. There wasn't time to do anything else. I don't blame them at all.'

Did I say this to hide my jealousy at the care now lavished on orphans? It was a distinct possibility.

There were four doors that led away from the hall. First door on the right took you into the old dining room. It is a sitting room now but back in our time this was where we ate breakfast and tea, and lunch, if it was a school holiday.

At the time, five dining tables dominated the room. A member of staff sat at the head of each one.

Barry was at the head of mine and Des's.

'I'll always remember how I hated cheese on toast with a passion,' Des said, 'but one day you told me to put brown sauce on it and since then I've loved it. Every time I eat that I think of you.'

I was touched. It was always the little details that made the bigger impact.

Des recalled the seating arrangements and suddenly the names of our ghosts spilled out from his lips.

Julie and Rebecca over there, Maggie over there, Mothy over there, David there, Terry there, Norman the boy who stuttered here, Ann and Anais there.

This room had another memory for me.

I remembered being called into it one Sunday afternoon when I was twelve years old and Barry and Julie sitting at a table and telling me not to worry, that all would be okay, that I was special and they would never leave me, that they would be at the Home for as long as it took to get me to university.

And I recalled thinking how strange this pledge was. I had not asked for it nor even thought about the pair of them leaving Burbank.

I should have known something was up then.

At that time I was settled, and not because of Barry and Julie but because of my fellow Burbankians. They had saved my life. There was Big Tommy and his brother Frank, then Terry, Graham and Jimmy B.

They were older than me and smarter and wilder. I didn't particularly get on with all of them but they accepted me, made me feel wanted. I was ten years old and it was one of the first times in my life that I had been made to feel this way. It was a valuable feeling. I felt safe in their company, truly looked after.

I saw that in them which the rest of the world could or would not. I saw their humanity. That made me blessed.

Ironically, it was in this room that Barry and Julie fell apart. One tea time Barry sat at the table, brooding. He and Julie had argued badly.

Finally, Barry snapped. He rose in a fury, went to Julie's table, picked up a bowl of rice pudding and smeared it onto the head of a girl sitting at her table.

Then he strode out of the room. A minute later we heard his car start up and screech away down the drive, heading for the pub, heading for oblivion.

The girl sat in shock, rice pudding dripping down onto her curiously small ears. But we all knew that Barry did not intend to put a bowl over her head. It was Julie's head he wanted.

Later on in life, a conservatory was built onto the side of this dining room. It acted as a second but very small sitting room. There was a TV and a record player, a couple of chairs. The smaller kids never really went in there but I sat in there for hours and hours.

I watched *Fawlty Towers* here, and got so obsessed with *The Sweeney*, it actually hurt me to miss an episode. I fell in love with Brian Moore the football commentator, and swooned to The Persuaders who dressed in clothes I thought I would never be able to afford. But I was wrong.

I watched every episode of *Top of the Pops* in this room, and later on, *The Old Grey Whistle Test*. This is where I fell in love with certain bands – The Faces, Genesis, Bowie, Lindisfarne, T. Rex.

But my one over-riding memory of this room was sitting by the record player playing one particular song over and over again – *The Long and Winding Road* by The Beatles.

I was thirteen and that song moved me like no other and did so for years. Later on in life, I wondered how Paul McCartney had managed to tap so vividly into the orphan's soul. How had he done that? I kept wondering until I read Paul McCartney lost his mother when he was just eleven years old.

I think he carried that sadness around with him until the day he sat down and God gave him those opening chords and that opening line.

The song is not just about sadness and loss but it is also about love and light and beauty, symbolised by the wild and windy night that the rain washes away. That song spoke to my soul and it still does. Even now, I find so much solace in those words and that music.

'Come on,' I said, to Des and Gary, 'onwards.'

We left the dining room and went into the kitchen.

On the right was a very large oven and over in the left hand corner, a walk-in larder, where loaves of cheap bread and countless jars of Robertson's marmalade once lived.

'God, I had forgotten about that,' Des suddenly exclaimed.

He pointed to a room to the right which had been built onto the original house and sometimes acted as either a sitting room or a staff bedroom.

I felt a little jolt in my stomach. In 1975, my social worker took me into that room and told me, as best she could, that the man I had been told all my life was my father was not.

He was a lie, cooked up by the authorities to cover up the true circumstances of my birth. My father did not live in Canada as I had been told. He was not the man who had fathered my two sisters. My father was a ghost, a real ghost. No one knew his name, his identity.

That day will always live with me. I remember I sat there in that gloomy fading afternoon light, taking in this shocking information and thinking to myself, God, haven't you done enough? Haven't I taken enough blows in life without having to deal with this? You take me away from my mother and give me a foster mother who beats me senseless. Then you place me in a home.

Now you tell me that I have been lied to all these years, that I have no idea who my true father is. What did I do to gain such favours?

For weeks after, I moved slowly. I kept thinking to myself, they have made a mistake.

My social worker will come back to Burbank and sit me down and say we are so sorry the files were switched, a secretary messed up, this hasn't happened to you. We got the wrong boy, everything is good, everything is as it should be.

We are so sorry to have upset you. Here take this money, buy whatever you want.

I seemed to spend a lot of my time in care daydreaming in such a fashion, always thinking that the wrongs in my life would be magically corrected and I would be returned to normality. And in these dreams, sunshine and lemonade were always present, always, and I don't know why.

But it never happened. Every day dawned and every day closed, and no one came and no one apologised. A month I spent in gloom and then I snapped. I used the orphan's fuck you.

Why should I let liars and deceivers ruin me? I am not going to give you that satisfaction. I am going to carry on as normal and this whole affair can melt away into the background and stay there for all I care. And that is what I did and that is how I put a smile back on my face and a spring into my footstep.

I went over and I opened the door and peered inside. I took a deep breath and I closed the door.

And as I did I saw my ghost stand up from that chair and fly out of the window.

I turned and moved through a door which led into the old cloakroom. Des and Gary followed me through.

This is where we hung our school blazers, polished and kept our shoes.

I glanced at the bench and saw myself sitting there in my school uniform, my eyes greedily scanning the *Daily Mirror*, consumed by the football reports, fascinated by the picture of Peter Wilson, their sports writer, thinking how great must it be to have such a job.

And many years later I got one just like it myself. But I was unhappy the whole time and knew then and first-hand the power of illusion: You are in the paper, you are on TV, you must be fine, oh so fine.

The door of the room led out into a small courtyard, the space where the staff hung our bed sheets and clothes and as they blew like crazy in the autumn wind, we loved to run through them, and then down the back drive to the garden.

Today, sheets are still being hung here. Des and I both smile at this picture. Some part of our world remains the same.

It was also here that I first proved myself to the gang by mounting a bicycle and hurtling down the back drive across the main drive and then flying into the garden at about ten feet high before landing successfully.

It was not the fact that I had successfully completed the mission, it was the fact that I had taken it on in the first place that won me respect and friendship. Another valuable lesson.

Then I noticed a locked gate at the end of the wall. I walked over to it with growing excitement.

This was the boiler room where we spent so many hours smoking and talking. This is where Frank V. once said to me, 'You know Paolo, it don't get any worse than this,' and I absorbed those words and even if they lay dormant for years, I now see that it was their truth that helped push me onwards.

For if Frank's words were true, then I only had one place to go – upward.

I looked down at the bottom of those stairs and barely made out the lumpy grey boiler that once heated the whole house.

Suddenly, I heard the boiler ignite and a thousand memories rushed up the stairs towards me.

I saw Jimmy B. teaching me to punch the dirty dark walls so as to toughen up my hands for fighting. I recalled the dark coal powder that smeared our hands and how, when I gazed upon it, I was reminded of the books I had read containing little orphan boys who were chimney sweeps.

I thought of the girls we enticed here, hoping to push eager tongues into their mouths, fumbling with their buttons, and how sometimes a few of them did not wriggle away from us, and how some let me do what I wanted and how very special that made me feel because I was wanted.

So much resided in that darkened room it really was quite incredible.

'It's a bit cold out here,' Des said.

I dragged myself away from the gate and followed him and Gary back inside.

We went through the back door and into the old playroom.

A piano once stood in the corner of this room. I thought of other pianos I had seen in other houses, other places, and they all had something ours didn't – photographs. People place photographs on piano tops. Ours was bare.

Des had a camera, as did some staff members, but in truth there were few photographic records of my time in Burbank. My photographs were songs and books and certain items of clothing and footballers and smells, such as that of newly cut grass; those were the things that triggered the memories which will never be eradicated, not pictures.

The playroom. We stand in wonder. I reminded Des of the chest of drawers that used to stand by the door and how every year he would dump his Christmas presents there.

'I hated Christmas here,' I told him.

'I didn't,' he said. 'I liked it.'

I was taken aback. I always presumed Des and I felt the same way on every matter. We moved as one, remember?

'Really?' I said. 'I found it horrible, waking up and going downstairs to get useless presents.'

'Those gifts were crap,' Des agreed. 'Things like socks and slippers, crap stuff. But I'm not talking about that bit. I'm talking about later on in the day. Don't you remember how the staff wouldn't let us into the dining room after lunch? How we had to stay away from the dining room all afternoon? And then at five o'clock they opened up the door and the room had been transformed? Don't you remember that? I'll never forget it. It was magical.

'The tables were taken out, chairs put around the wall, candles lit, and special lighting and decorations installed. And then there was a large table, a great buffet of treats with pork pies and sausage rolls and crisps and coca cola, food which had been denied us the rest of the year.

'Then Barry announced that Father Christmas had delivered more gifts,' he continued. 'But these presents were different to the morning one. They were personalised and thoughtful. I remember I got a lovely pen and you would get something like a really beautiful book or an album you wanted. Don't you remember? God your memory is bad.

'Then we would go into the main sitting room and sit in a circle and play games. Barry sat at the piano and he sang songs such as, On 'is 'orse with 'is 'awk in 'is 'and and then Empsie, a friend of Barry and Julie's, would perform a number which always ended with a fearful scream and we would all jump up in fright. Don't you remember any of this?'

Suddenly, Des's Christmas past appeared in front of me.

I remembered how I sat on the floor by Nan's chair. She was Julie's mum and she would slyly slip me her glass of snowball and I would take a sip and I would hand it back and she would smile, and so would I because it was our secret and it made me feel special. It made me feel wanted.

I remembered also that there was no fighting and no arguing between us kids that day, nor was there trouble with any of the staff. It was just thirty human beings of all ages, from all different places in the world, sitting in a room, joined as one.

Des's enthusiasm moved me. He was right. It had been a good day. The staff had done their very best for us, had made it a time to remember. Their work, their care, it had counted for something.

I felt vaguely ashamed I had never acknowledged this before.

As we left the playroom and moved back into the hallway we had entered, I noted one of the kid's CDs. It was by Puff Daddy.

'Tell whoever owns this,' I said cheekily to Gary, 'that there's loads of better rap stuff out there than this guy.'

'I will do,' Gary said. 'He might not listen, though. He's eight years old. Shall we go upstairs?'

We walked upwards, reached a small landing.

Des pointed to a part of the floor and laughed.

'Remember that?' he asked.

'No.'

'You came home so drunk one night you couldn't make it to your bed which was about ten feet away from here. So you simply laid down on the floor here and went to sleep.'

In my final years at Burbank I got drunk quite a few times. I loved the way alcohol loosened my tongue, allowed me to express the thoughts that I kept strictly caged for fear of ridicule and exposure to others.

Of course, I hated the time spent yearning for sleep as the ceiling above whirred round so fast you thought it would never stop, and your stomach churned and your head throbbed. But that sensation of freeing yourself from yourself and the chains inside exhilarated.

Drugs never really made it into our world. At Burbank, the only drug I could recall being used on a regular basis was shoe perfumer. I tried it one night, got dizzy, coughed a lot, and told the guy who had given it to me that I was really high. But I wasn't.

People-pleasing at its finest, people.

We moved across the landing and into our old bedroom. Des and I gasped. One bed stood in the centre of the room. One bed. On the small cabinet next to it there was a clock, a DVD player, a stereo unit, a radio and a big TV.

Des and I were speechless. I turned to Gary.

'Only one kid sleeps here?' I asked.

'Yes,' he replied as if I had just asked is it true that humans need air to breathe. 'Why do you sound so surprised?'

'Because eight kids slept in this room,' I answered, 'including myself and Des.'

'How on earth did you get eight in here?' Gary asked.

'Simple,' Des replied. 'Six kids in single beds, four along that wall, two along that wall and then two kids in a bunk bed in that corner over there.'

Gary swallowed this information slowly. There was silence. I broke it.

'And we did not have an alarm clock let alone a TV and a radio and whatever else he has got there. Orphans today,' I said to Des, 'they don't know they're born.'

'Actually they are called looked after kids now,' Gary said and I nearly snapped back that no one – no one – had the right to tell me what to call myself.

But I bit the tongue and tried to recall where my bed was placed.

I think it was to the right and third along. It was important. This was the room where the Home's routine began. Seven in the mornings sharp a staff member came into the room and shouted at us, and we stumbled out of our beds and went into the nearby bathroom and splashed water on our faces.

Back in the room, we dressed in clothes, either bought at a local cheap shop or donated to the Home by kindly souls. Every morning, all of us rag dolls walked to school in black trousers with the knees frayed, horrible white nylon shirts and shapeless blazers.

Which was fine, until I got to thirteen, and my friends started dressing in the Suedehead fashion, and they arrived at school beautiful in their white Ben Shermans and their black Sta-Prest trousers, and their loafers so shiny.

They looked like young men, young adults, and I felt so inadequate in their company. So feeble.

I nearly died in this bedroom. After Laz and I robbed Woking Football Club and had been caught, I contracted bad pneumonia. It was the second time this illness had invaded me. The first time was at Mrs K.'s when my temperature soared to 104. The second time around my temperature hit exactly the same number. I spent two weeks in a haze and then recovered. Close run thing. Get to 106 and it's addio.

I smartened up after the illness. Barry told me that school had seriously considered my expulsion. I swallowed hard at that revelation, for that was a punishment I had to avoid. To lose my friends there would have taken me to a place I knew I was not strong enough to visit.

Yet this bedroom was also a happy place. Love and laughter lived here. This is where friendships were made and strengthened, eight boys in a room, eight boys in thin pyjamas and thin beds, unable to resist the temptation to disturb the stillness that hovered above us, breaking the hush with whispered conversations that furtively darted around the room, issued from one bed to another and then back again.

Stories about the staff, stories about girls, stories from school, stories from the world outside the Home's grounds, stories about neighbours and local characters, stories from television shows, but never stories of one's past, never stories about your life, or stories that expressed the reason for your presence in this darkened room.

Sometimes the words were angry, threatening – 'I'll get you in the morning, I fucking will' – other times you had to bury your face in the thin pillow to stifle the laughter that would alert the staff, rouse their anger. And then before sleep finally arrived, trying to gaze through the crack of the curtain to see a star, to see a full moon, find something, anything, that would tell you that tomorrow would come, uncertain in nature, but always on time.

'Shall we go?' Gary asked.

Behind us was Barry and Julie's bedroom, the room we never saw or entered, as sacred to us as an altar in a church. The only time I knocked on its door I was in bits, tears scalding my face.

Mothy had bullied me for over a year and I could take no more. Although he had told me he would kill me if I split on him I simply didn't care. 'Kill me,' I cried and I ran to Barry's bedroom door and I knocked on it and Barry opened it, in surprise. No one knocked on his door.

'You have to help me,' I cried. 'Mothy keeps beating me up.'

And I told him of the beatings, the terrible beatings that had taken place.

'I'm sure it's not that bad,' Barry said. I couldn't believe his words.

Could he not see the true terrible story painted upon my face, drawn there in tears and painful gulps? Actually, he did. Soon after Mothy was moved to another Home and life turned better for me.

We moved on. I glanced to my right and saw three rooms. One was a toilet.

I recalled sitting on that toilet one Sunday morning reading my book and staff member Maggie Patterson ripping open the door and grabbing the book off me and repeatedly slamming it onto my head, crying, 'Do not read on the toilet,' and I sat there and as I took the blows, I thought, but why are you hitting me? Reading is good. Don't you know that?

The room to the left was Barry and Julie's bathroom. The room opposite the bedroom I shared with David Westbrook.

I was fifteen when I was given that room and I remembered it fondly.

Music and books and football consumed me. That's all I cared about. They took me out of the past and the future and placed me right in the present.

All I had to do was to sit by the record player in my bedroom and read and listen and sing along to my favourite band – probably The Faces at that point – and suddenly I had no memories to taunt and haunt me. I could submerge myself into different worlds and fantasies and turn the world bright and beautiful.

I had a good time in that room.

I also recalled vividly standing outside Barry's bathroom every morning and hearing him cough and retch up the result of the previous night's cigarettes and alcohol. We didn't know at the time he drank so heavily, had no idea. He was clever like that, able to cover up his vices and act normally. Only Julie his wife knew the full extent and she was hardly going to call him out on it. It could mean losing her marriage and therefore her job.

We moved on, upwards to the top floor of the Home.

There were four bedrooms on this floor, plus a toilet.

We walked into the boy's bedroom and went through to the back room.

Instantly, Des and I thought of Rod, the brother he and I shared for so many years. Rod was unlike Des. He didn't read, wasn't that bothered by school.

Sure he liked football, music, girls but for Rod money was the most important thing ever. Nothing else mattered. He was obsessed with the stuff.

I differed, I believed in art. Music and books were the way to reach happiness. Not the filthy lucre, that was fool's gold.

Hour after hour, Rod and I went at each other, argued our corner until finally we made a pact. We swore that in twenty years' time wherever we were in the world we would meet up in a pub and see who was the happiest and therefore who was right.

Twenty years later, in Guildford, we met up. Des was there too.

Rod had gone into the building game, was very successful. Lived nearby in a big house with his wife and kids, worked every day, maintained a large bank account. He had read my book *The Looked After Kid* and was nonchalant about it.

'It was all right,' he said when I asked, 'it was okay.'

Unlike me, the past was something Rod paid little attention to. He called his childhood, 'a book I have put on the shelf. It's there and if I want to get it down I will. So far I haven't felt the need.'

Which is why he didn't want to be interviewed for this book. I had no problem with that. He had to do what was right for him. Vive la différence.

'So Rod,' I said slyly, 'remember the conversations about money and art, how you went on about money and I went on about art?'

'I know,' he said brightly, 'and you know what? Fuck money. I chased it and I got it. In fact I have got loads of it. Can make you some if you want, it's easy to do, no big deal. Do you know what I would really like to do?'

'No.'

'I would like to write a book.'

I smiled big time at that one.

'Suppose you think you have won,' he said.

'No,' I said. 'I'm laughing because I chased the books and I got them. I have written many books now. But you know what?'

'What?'

'I'd love to make some money now.'

I raised my glass to my teenage brother. 'A draw,' I said.

'A draw,' he agreed and we clinked glasses.

I looked at the wall on the right and remembered a picture I had hung on it of David Bowie. I recalled lying on the bed for hours looking at that picture of him as Ziggy Stardust trying to work out what song he was playing at that exact moment in time, where he was, what he was thinking. I did the exact same thing with my poster of the Spurs centre forward Martin Chivers.

In the picture Martin was either receiving the ball or passing it. I spent hours wondering what game he was playing in and where the ball was going next and was he about to score and who were the opposition?

I never did get the answer but two years ago I met Chivers. My agent called me and said he wanted to write a biography and they were looking for a writer.

We met him at a hotel in London. I could hardly look at him. When my agent told him that he was a hero of mine, I actually blushed and looked away. I got to write the biography with him and throughout the whole time I spent with him in his car, in his home, I could never tell him about my past and what he meant to me.

Chivers once played for Southampton Football Club. In April 2009 we went there together to interview some of his old team mates, get information.

We caught the train from Waterloo. And it stopped at Woking. Burbank stood half a mile away. I could not believe it. For two minutes as Martin spoke, oblivious to my position, I sat there thinking to myself, My God if you had told me back in Burbank that at some point in my life I would be sat on a train in Woking with Martin Chivers I would have thought you were mad.

As the train slowly slid out of the station I said a little prayer, one of thanks, one of gratitude, that life could be as wondrous as this.

That book, his biography, started here in this bedroom.

I looked over to the small closed window, remembered Rod and I hanging out of it as we smoked Number Six cigarettes, blowing smoke into dark winter nights before we dived back into our beds when we heard a noise, feigning sleep, trying to bury nicotine breath into yet another painfully thin pillow.

Des laughed. 'You know what I remember best about this room? Being woken by Barry at all hours to keep him company as he went off to pick up kids who had run away, usually named Norman Bass, from various parts of Southern England.'

'You and Barry got on well didn't you?' I say. 'I found him hard to warm to.'

'I liked him. I know he had his faults, like pretending to go to the shops and then diving into the pub every evening but he was a good sort, Barry. He was usually all right with me.'

'Gone now, you know that don't you?' I ask.

'I know. I heard it was the drink that did for him,' Des said.

We left the boy's bedroom, went into the staff member's room. This room was so special to me. It had once been occupied by a young woman named Rosie. She was a hippy and she introduced me to so many new worlds, so many new experiences.

It was here that I read Jack Kerouac's *Town and Country* and thought it so much better than *On the Road*. It was here I read Hunter S. Thompson's *Fear and Loathing on the Campaign Trail*, and I knew it to be so much better than *Fear and Loathing in Las Vegas*. It was here I heard *Blood on the Tracks* by Bob Dylan and thought it to be the best album in the world.

'That woman gave me so much,' I told Des and Gary, 'I will never forget her.' She taught me that in this world there were a million other worlds and that no one world is better or worse than the other.

There was dignity in the road sweeper as there is in the professor. She hoped I would find my world and I did and in part because of her.

But I couldn't tell them everything she had given to me and it was then that I felt a piercing to the heart. For Rosie rests in peace now, struck down by MS.

She lived in south London then and I should have seen more of her. But I was on the run from my past and I so couldn't find the strength to cross the river. But Rosie knew me and she understood. Above all, she forgave.

On the landing we stood outside the bedroom the older girls once slept in. Des and Rod and I occasionally sneaked in here for midnight kisses and fumbles with girls who opened their lips, and occasionally their hearts.

But we did not say anything in front of Gary. It just did not feel right.

Instead, Des and I nodded at each other and in that gesture alone we knew.

And then it felt right to go.

We had seen our old home, exhausted the past.

There had been more laughter than sadness.

Burbank had dark memories for all of us but it also contained wonderful moments that in the passing of time have gained in strength and colour.

Burbank represented such a huge part of our lives that to feel bad every time you thought about it was a terrible life sentence to carry. I didn't want that for Des and I didn't want it for myself.

Life in Burbank had been tough. A child without love is always in a bad place. But life in Burbank had also been rich, exciting, adventurous, a life that very few people get to live.

I can only speak for myself and for the guys I had spoken to but I think Burbank made unique people of us all. I think care makes unique people of us all.

We said goodbye to Gary, headed down the drive towards the pub for food and refreshments. At the end of the drive I turned back to take one last look at the house and it was then that I saw a little boy come out of Burbank and look up at the sky.

Strange. There had been no children present during our visit.

Des and I turned out of the drive and began to ascend. We walked past the old post office where we spent so much of our pocket money on packs of cigarettes, and fashionable sweets, past the small houses, and we went up and up and up the hill.

At the top was a pub. Des went in and got drinks and I found us a table outside.

The day had broken now. God had decided in our favour and the sun was bearing through. I felt a warmth inside and outside of myself.

The morning had been one to remember. I had faced Burbank and no bad had come of it. I felt stronger now than I did when I woke up.

A good feeling.

Des brought the glasses to the table and we saluted each other.

The book, this journey, was now finished.

All that remained was for a question to be answered: had Care been a good thing for the guys? Had Burbank made or destroyed them?

I believe it had done both. All of us had been through the darkness. But more importantly it seemed that all of us had discovered a light we could happily live in.

Des had his work and his music. He had his freedom and that made him happy. Norman and David both had women they adored and work they loved. They also had children in their lives that they sought to make well and happy. And in doing so they healed themselves.

Terry too had love but he also had God. God gave him certainty. Faith had turned into his valuable ally.

Before Burbank, my life was a hell. I lived from the age of four to ten with a very sick woman who beat and humiliated me. At Burbank I found all the things that were absent from my life up until that point.

Love, friendship, warmth. Not once did I experience anything like that woman's cruelty at Burbank, except for maybe Mothy's bullying of me.

Yet despite that unhappy period, most of my memories of Burbank, of my teenage life in care, were positive.

Contrary to what you might believe about life in care, life there was not doom laden or stultifyingly miserable. Some days were, for sure, but weren't some of yours?

At Burbank, we were joined at the hip by our shattered childhoods. That made us as one. It did not matter where you came from, how you spoke, what you had been. We were all in it together and somehow – mystically, unconsciously – we recognised that fact and acted upon it, even if we never verbalised it.

At Burbank, I learnt to accept people for who they are, regardless of anything. That is a great quality to take into later life. I learnt not to judge people on their accents. I learnt not to discriminate.

At Burbank I learnt about the deep value of friendships. The giving, the taking, the creating of something meaningful and worthwhile between people. Friendships remained hugely important for me. The five closest friends I possess now, I have known collectively for over a hundred years.

I developed courage in Burbank. I have been braver in life because of my past, because of Burbank. I think it gave me an advantage. I was better equipped to realise my ambitions than others with parents. Why? Because I had no fear. What could you do to me that had not already been done? Nothing.

Remember Frank V.'s words. It don't get worse than this. So I shot for the stars and occasionally, I reached them.

My hope is that every child in care does so as well.

If I had learnt anything, it was the power of the human spirit to absorb blows so terrible that sometimes their fury and anger surpassed all incomprehension, and yet still be able to emerge into a light of safety and healing. To see that in Des, Norman, David and Terry, immensely moved me. I don't know why I use the past tense. It still moves me and it always will.

I finished my drink and stood. I said goodbye to Des with a hug and I left the bar.

I walked down the hill and the sun hit me and enveloped me in a special warmth. I stopped and took a last look at Burbank. As I gazed through the trees at that old familiar house, I was disturbed by a noise.

I looked and saw a small child walking down Burbank's driveway.

He was wearing a blazer, a white nylon shirt, a tie, scuffed up shoes and black trousers that were frayed at the knees.

I know the boy. I know him well. The boy is me aged twelve, walking to school in the early morning air. He is thinking about Teresa Driver, the record at number one, the book he has just read, thinking about the friends he is about to see and play football with, thinking about the lessons that lie ahead.

I stood back. And the boy passed. And as he did he looked up at me and he gave me the most beautiful smile on what was probably one of his most terrible days. And in that very instant my heart knew it was all truly meant to be.

Half an hour later, I boarded the silver train to London.

I settled in my seat and then realised something – I was on my way home.

Finally, I was going home.